RIGHT PRINCIPLES

A conservative philosophy of politics

Lincoln Allison

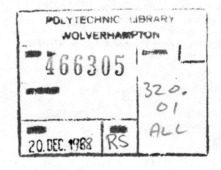
Basil Blackwell

© Lincoln Allison 1984

First published 1984
First published in paperback 1986

Basil Blackwell Ltd
108 Cowley Road, Oxford OX4 1JF, UK

Basil Blackwell Inc.
432 Park Avenue South, Suite 1505
New York, NY 10016, USA

British Library Cataloguing in Publication Data
Allison, Lincoln
  Right principles: a conservative philosophy
  of politics.
  1. Political science
  I. Title
  320'.01   JA71
  ISBN 0-631-13475-1
  ISBN 0-631-15032-3

Library of Congress Cataloging in Publication Data

Allison, Lincoln.
  Right principles.

  Bibliography: p.
  Includes index.
  1. Conservatism. 2. Political science. I. Title.
  JA66.A44   1984   320.5'2   84-11084
  ISBN 0-631-13475-1
  ISBN 0-631-15032-3

Typeset by Oxford Verbatim Limited
Printed in Great Britain by
The Bath Press, Avon

CONTENTS

INTRODUCTION

This is not a book about political philosophy; it is a book of political philosophy. Since the difference is not obvious, as it would be with poetry, nor meaningless, as it would be with history, it is as well to make the distinction explicit. This is not a history of conservative thought, nor a survey of contemporary conservativism. I would not claim any kind of role or status as a spokesman for conservativism.

The book is a personal explication of certain philosophical problems which are directly or indirectly related to politics. Some of its subject matter, like 'rights', 'liberty' and 'power', is unambiguously central to the concerns of anybody who calls himself a political theorist or political philosopher. Other topics, like religion, science and language, remain essential considerations for anyone who would be a political philosopher in the broadest sense. My aim in writing the book was to produce a coherent account of the main topics and problems in political philosophy. The result is recognisably conservative, both as a whole and, usually, in the details of its parts. I make no claim that it is *the* conservative philosophy of politics: as I have to make clear in chapter 1, there are several quite different and often opposing philosophical approaches which are compatible with political conservatism as it is recognised in England in the late twentieth century. This is one interpretation of one of them, though, naturally, I believe it is the best interpretation of the best of all philosophical traditions.

There is no need for me to apologise for the political commitment of the book. Such commitment is currently fashionable in political philosophy, and conservative political theory, though it has begun the process of catching up, is very under-represented compared with liberal, radical and marxist theory. In any case, much of the commitment in this book is purely negative; it consists of a belief in the incoherence of much that is believed. In some ways it would be fair to describe the lines of argument developed as a political anti-theory rather than a theory. I would not be happy, though, with describing them as a political anti-philosophy because this might be thought to imply an opposition to the logical and linguistic dissection of arguments. This distinction between 'philosophy' and 'theory' is not one which is clearly implied by current academic usage, however. There, 'political theory' and 'political philosophy' overlap to the point of interchangeability, an overlap which I generally accept in using the terms.

The book is an essay in conservatism, but much more fundamentally than that it is an essay in conceptual scepticism. At its simplest (and it frequently suffices even at its simplest) conceptual scepticism says that political values and concepts are incoherent: they do not mean anything, at least in the serious sense of 'mean' which requires clarity and substance. As applications of this I will be arguing, for instance, that a belief in human equality is not a belief at all, in any serious sense; that a belief in justice can amount to anything at all and that proposals for the redistribution of power in society are necessarily either empty or deceitful.

The relationship between conceptual scepticism and conservatism is not a necessary one. It would be possible to accept the main arguments of this book and still believe in a substantive political programme which was recognisably 'left wing'. However it would not be possible to accept these arguments and still believe that the canons of left-wing belief, both traditional and fashionable, were *true*. In other words I am not particularly arguing against those who say that, for instance, 'The House of Lords should be abolished because its abolition would have the following constitutional advantages . . .' or 'I believe that people should be able to publish what they choose in any context they are able to . . .' though I happen to disagree with both of those proposals. What I am attacking is those who argue that 'the House of Lords should be abolished because it is undemocratic' or 'censorship should be abolished because it is incompatible with freedom.' However, anyone who managed to be both a conceptual sceptic and a left-winger would have to have a bizarre set of values or, perhaps, a bizarre sense of humour; most of the left-wing belief is in words, in abstract ideals, rather than in specific recommendations. It would be as eccentric to believe in universal comprehensive education without believing in 'equality' as I think it would be to believe in chastity without believing in God.

I do not, of course, expect to 'win' the argument about politics in the sense that people in general will come to talk and act as if conceptual scepticism were substantially correct. Political theory (or philosophy) is a small and refined part of the whole body of talk about politics; a book is just a small drop in the ocean of discourse. I do believe that some of the sceptical arguments I will put in this book are valid and demonstrable, but the forces ranged against them are enormously strong. Political words have a rhetorical power; they move people. In many cases the words cannot be tied down to precise criteria nor translated into programmes of action, but they conjure up images and make the heart beat faster; they solicit support and they unite people into movements. Many words are also 'obsessive' : they express a desire to ask questions which fit attractive images rather than the real world. However convincingly I may argue that 'God' and 'democracy' are words which denote no particular concept, people will still want to know what God is like or what constitutes a true democracy. The number of people who want to make statements which have the properties of clarity, meaning and truth is very small indeed compared with the number who want to answer questions like these. Though a book may be a drop in the ocean, authors are still entitled to their traditional hope that the drop will create ripples which will, eventually, make their mark on the whole ocean.

Conceptual scepticism is my basis for conservatism, which makes me an intellectual descendent of Hume rather than of Burke, Locke or Hobbes. I draw also on other strains such as conservative pessimism and certain recognisably conservative values. But these do not constitute the main theme of the argument. Other bases of conservatism provide political allies, but not necessarily intellectual agreement except on the question of unacceptability of those movements, programmes and principles which conservatives oppose. Otherwise there is no necessary connection, for instance, between the arguments in this book and the policies of the Conservative Party. Nor can any such gap be analysed in terms of the difference (in current jargon) between 'wet' and 'dry' conservatives. As I argue in chapter 1, there are many kinds of conservative and many bases for conservatism. To divide them all into 'wet' and 'dry' is about as useful as insisting that all domestic animals are sheep or cows, which necessarily leads to a lot of silly arguments about which category a goat falls into. Sometimes a taxonomy can be so bad that it is better not to have one at all.

Like every author, I want the whole world to read my book but, more realistically, it is directed towards two markets. First, it is intended to be read by undergraduate students following courses in political 'analysis', 'philosophy', 'concepts' and 'theory' (not including courses in the history of political theory). It offers them an approach to the problems which is undeniably different and (I hope) more coherent than those already available. It is also aimed at more general readers who might be interested to read a philosophical basis of conservatism. In two separate ways, it offers to balance the existing literature. First, to increase the proportion of conservative argument within contemporary political theory but also to offer an alternative form of conservatism to those already available which are dominated by such aliens (to my approach) as liberals, Hegelians and Christians. Not that I am to be construed as attacking these approaches : a conservative should be wise enough to know the difference between philosophical agreement and political alliance and to appreciate the value of both. Let our enemies break up over a premise here or an inference there; we have no need.

Finally comes the need to justify, or at least show awareness of, one's shortcomings. A number of important political concepts are not directly dealt with in this book. Apart from the question of length, different reasons apply to the most notable omissions. The concept of 'politics' itself is not specifically considered, partly because I do not consider it very interesting, but also because I have discussed it elsewhere. 'Interests' is absent even though I do not consider it a very important concept; I have left it out because the issues which lie at the core of arguments about interests – questions about persons, their wants, the conditions under which they can be said to be mistaken about themselves and their wants, the ways in which they can be conditioned and controlled – are discussed in other chapters, mainly chapters 9 and 10. The state is also omitted; I do not believe that it matters very much how we treat the word 'state' and what we believe the nature of the state to be. The current revival in theorising about the state consists mainly of putting old arguments under new topic headings.

Those who judge the worth of a book by its footnotes will notice that there are none here and draw their conclusions accordingly. The book stands or falls as a statement of political and philosophical arguments. Quotations from, and references to, other works are included only because they are so well known they cannot be ignored, or merely as an example of a common form of argument, or because they said it better than I could. In most cases the works referred to are extremely well known and, anyway, my argument is never dependent on a particular quotation. Books or articles (whichever are more appropriate) are referred to in the text, so that a determined reader could go to the source of the quotation. I have excluded notes partly for the negative reason that they add nothing to my argument, but also as a symbol of what I intend, which is to write my own political philosophy and not to survey or categorise other people's, nor to prove to anybody how many books I have read. I have appended a bibliography of works to which reference is made in the text, indicating how general or specific each reference to any author is.

1

VARIETIES OF CONSERVATISM

Marx wrote for over 40 years, sometimes as a scholar, sometimes as a polemicist, sometimes as a journalist. Within his scholarly writings the emphasis moved from philosophy to sociology to economics. Marx had his own method of study, his own view of the main course that history was taking and his own approach to the relationship between scholarship and commitment. He made original contributions to sociology and economics. In common with most other social commentators he used crucial terms, like 'class' and 'alienation', in a shifting and ambiguous way. Some aspects of social understanding, such as a theory of the state, were left inexplicit and undeveloped. He died over a century ago; since his death the world has changed faster than ever before, many of his expectations have been confounded and a bewildering variety of states and social movements have cited Marx's name. They include the violent and the non-violent, the permissive and the puritanical, the conservative and the radical. Some insist that to be a Marxist is to believe a set of related doctrines which were expounded by Marx; others, including many contemporary 'Eurocommunists', say that it is only feasible to share Marx's spirit of approach or to be part of a developing intellectual and moral tradition in which Marx is the leading figure.

Thus, it is very difficult to be a Marxist and even more difficult to tell a Marxist from a non–Marxist or convincingly to translate your Marxism into a prescription for action in the late twentieth century. There are overlapping difficulties in being a 'socialist' and parallel and similar difficulties in being a 'Christian'. It is both more difficult again and also easier to be a conservative. The sense in which it is easier is that conservatism as a movement is not defined or inspired by moral or intellectual precepts at all. I should make it clear that when I talk about conservatives I am talking primarily about English conservatives and that I am treating the terms 'conservative' and 'Tory' as synonyms. Some of what I say will have implications for conservatism in other places. Distinctions are often made between Tories and conservatives, but the different distinctions simply contradict one another and there is no way of making such a distinction which is both established and coherent.

Much conservatism is defined and motivated by the defence of established interests. There is no real problem about distinguishing between interests and principles. Both are kinds of want. Interests are derived from those wants which are self-orientated, ultimately explicable in terms of benefits to the person having the want or to a limited and definable group of which he is a member. Principles are publicly orientated wants, they are desires for a state of affairs the benefits of which are only explicable in terms of an indefinite number of people, such as society, humanity or creation. Thus we can distinguish between political movements which are primarily driven by principle and those primarily driven by interests. Most movements involve both; support for the preservation of the countryside or the subsidising of the arts, for example, could easily be either.

Whereas the great bulk of socialism or liberalism can only be understood, in terms of this distinction, as movements of principle, much conservatism is self-interested. Individually people join conservative organisations to make contacts, to further their careers or to find wealthy spouses. Much of what binds conservatives together is the desire to protect shared and established interests. This does not require shared or established doctrines or principles. The businessman who believes that life ought to be made easier for businessmen seeks allies; it does not matter very much to him whether his allies share his fundamental moral precepts, nor, indeed, whether they have any.

So there is truth in the common judgement that whereas most political movements have ideals (in the sense of broad desires for the welfare of man or society), conservatism does not. Certainly, there are parts of the Labour Movement which are equally unconcerned with ideals and at least equally preoccupied with the defence of established interests, but I mean 'movements' in the sense that socialism is a movement whereas the 'Labour Movement' is a mere alliance which incorporates some easily recognisable conservatives. There is also some truth in the common allegation that conservatism is a singularly 'selfish' approach. But conservatives are entitled to comment that there are many things worse than selfishness and that much of the worst destruction and malice in history was motivated by genuine principles. They might add, too, that since they attribute less importance to ideas than any other major political persuasion, they are more likely to sustain genuine moral and intellectual tolerance. Only a conservative ruler can, like Frederick the Great, make an agreement with his people that they can say what they like if he can do what he likes. It can also be said of conservatives that they are essentially negative. There is a profound and philosophical dimension to this negativism, but, for the moment, I mean only that when it does come to principles, conservatives know what they are against: they are against principles which threaten stability, their own economic interests, and those traditions and practices which their instincts tell them cannot be improved. This puts them against most principles and nearly all coherently ordered bodies of principle; there is unlikely to be a set of coherent and fundamental principles which justify the real condition of any society, let alone English society.

Thus conservatism is, in two senses, anti-intellectual. First, conservatives do not respect or value theories, preferring instead practice, experience and intuition. Whereas for most approaches to politics theory logically precedes action and for Marxists, theory and action are inextricably linked, theory follows action for many conservatives. It offers, at best, justification; at worst, it is time-wasting, confusing and subversive. It is all very well for Keynes (and many others) to say that the 'practical man' is an impossibility, that we must all hold theories, however implicitly. The difference remains that practical men may hold 'theories', in a sense, but unlike theoretical men they do not value or indulge the urge to work those theories out in an ordered and logical way. The test of the argument depends on what you mean by theory.

In a second sense, 'conservatives' and 'intellectuals' are all but opposites. One aspect of the intellectual in modern society, both in the way he sees himself and in the way others see him, is his 'role'. It is the intellectual's job to be critical; he must try to be 'relevant'. Vision, passion, commitment, anger are, therefore, the trademarks of the intellectual in an industrial or post-industrial society. He is no mere 'man of ideas', playing with theories because he finds them less ugly, less boring or less dirty than practice. This essentially 'committed' conception of the intellectual dominates much of the life of the mind in contemporary England. It is especially strong in (for example) sociology and the theatre. It specifically excludes conservatism in any proper sense.

The anti-intellectual status of conservatism can be a supreme strategic advantage. It is comparatively rare for conservatives to desert the Conservative Party because it is failing to live up to its principles. The debilitating schisms so common in other political movements can often be ignored. They exist, of course. I have seen rooms full of conservatives briefly, but intensely, divide on many issues of principle. Take development control in the sense of the state closely regulating what people do with their own land and buildings. Is it an excellent and indispensable institution or exactly what we are against? The authoritarian regime of Lee Kuan Yew in Singapore: the sort of thing we most admire or most abhor? Somehow the differences do not matter much. Conservatives say, 'We'll never see eye to eye on that one, old chap', and do little to further their own view. They easily accept leadership with very different principles from their own, provided it is effective in defeating 'them'.

Given this context, it would be tempting to abandon any attempt to make conservative ideas profound and explicit. Conservatives have no ideas; they merely use ideas. Most of the time, they are against ideas. They should confine themselves to what they do well: making and spending money and winning elections.

Fortunately, this is only one dimension of conservatism. Conservatives do have ideas. They are profound, subtle, diverse and distinctly conservative. Practical conservatives may spend little time on them, but without them conservatism would not only be difficult to justify, it would be impossible to take seriously.

SOME CONSERVATIVE IDEAS

Conservative thinking draws on a range of ideas which are dramatically different from each other in style and origin. I can best explain these by distinguishing between four main strands.

The Tory cosmology

Perhaps the predominant view of man and society over the range of literate societies so far has been that of the ordered hierarchy in which everything and every person has its place and corresponding duties. This is the vision of the universe which is, in Pope's great metaphor, a 'vast chain of Being, which from God began . . . .' It is a view of the universe which has a great appeal, of nostalgia if nothing else. It not only stresses the more attractive features of the past; it was how most people learned to see the world as children. In the Tory cosmology, understanding is worship and goodness acceptance.

> All Nature is but Art, unknown to thee
> All Chance, Direction, which thou canst not see.

But God is an absolute necessity of this vision. If it has any moral force (and sometimes it is mere poetry) it lies in keeping people in their place, preventing them from instigating rebellion. But why accept a difficult or humble place without divine sanction? The argument that it is 'natural' to do so means nothing – or rather it means several dozen different things – unless nature is elevated into a supernatural will and source of obligation and punishment: into God, in other words.

In England (as opposed to, say, Byzantium) people have been ill-disposed to accept Pope's conclusion that 'Whatever is, is RIGHT.' The greatest formal statement of Tory cosmology, Filmer's *Patriarcha*, an account of God, kings and peoples in a great bond of family obligation, was written during the long seventeenth-century struggle between king and parliament. But it was out of date when it was written. Although John Locke devoted a great deal of energy to refuting it, nothing like it was ever again to be treated as the basis of government, even by governments. Authority had supporters of a more contemporary and powerful nature, like Hobbes.

The Tory cosmology was never really the basis of conservatism in England as it was in many of the Catholic countries of continental Europe. It had little appeal in a country which abandoned serfdom and embraced capitalism and protestantism more quickly than any other. It is difficult to read the history of England from 1400 to 1900 and see the Tory cosmology as the basic framework of either argument or action.

However, ideas linger on in many parts of a culture other than formal philosophical and political dispute. The Tory cosmology was still a natural assumption for many in the eighteenth century when Pope wrote and when Bentham attacked natural law. Darwin dealt it another savage blow in 1859 when he published the *Origin of Species*, but like other intellectual thunderclaps its echoes and effects reverberated for many years. One of the most striking popular statements of the Tory cosmology was the 'sociological' verse of 'All things bright and beautiful'.

> The rich man in his castle,
> The poor man at his gate,
> God made them, high and lowly,
> And ordered their estate.

It was only in 1922 that this verse was taken out of *Hymns Ancient and Modern*, thus removing the last ideological obstacle to the quest for individual economic and social self-improvement which was, by then, universally accepted as praiseworthy. Since then the most well-known exponent of the Tory cosmology has been a television character, Alf Garnett in Johnny Speight's *Till Death Us Do Part*. Otherwise, statements of the Tory cosmology linger on in eccentric sermons and in the nature columns of newspapers. It remains a way of looking at the world which has some appeal to ordinary people but which is difficult to take seriously at the level of philosophical debate.

Marketism

There could scarcely be a range of ideas more different from the vision of the Tory cosmology than those which I am grouping together as 'marketism'. The former sees man as part of a great seemless web of things; out of context he has no meaning, no real existence. Acceptance is his normal and proper moral response. But most of the ideas associated with modernity and capitalism take the individual as their starting point. People exist: to talk of societies is only to imply a necessary abstraction, a way of talking about the relationships between individuals. Governments can only be justified insofar as they benefit individuals; their performance must be measured by their aggregate efficacity in doing so. The only purpose for which individuals can be said to exist is the satisfaction of wants; the uniquely efficient means for people to pursue their interests is the market, the regulated exchange of goods and services. The state must be understood as a hypothetical contract or agreement between citizens: choice, not acceptance, is the proper basis of our relationship to the universe. Voting is the appropriate way of ordering societies, at least beyond a certain level of development.

Marketism is the most modern and fully developed of man's accounts of man. In religion, whether in atheism or in protestantism, it asserts the primacy of the conscience. Morally it judges all action by its effects and all effects as they work upon the self: self-help, self-development, self-awareness, self-realisation. In art it is most typically represented by the ethos of art for art's sake, production being measured by the satisfaction it creates rather than by conformance to a higher moral purpose. In international relations, 'self-determination' is the basic principle. The economic aspects have reached very high levels of sophistication; the whole foundation of economics – indifference curves, preference theory and preference logic – are a vast and finely tuned development of the ideas of 'wanting' and 'choosing'.

As with many other 'isms', marketism exists in a strong version and a range of weak versions. By the strong version I mean that very clear relation, with prescriptive consequences, between the autonomous individual, the minimal state and the consequent market which is often called 'classical', 'laissez-faire' or 'nineteenth-century' liberalism. The high period of this doctrine in England was in the mid-nineteenth century. It was the 'prevailing ideology' of the country in a number of ways: it dominated the highest levels of theoretical debate and it served the interests of those who had economic power. But it was never wholly accepted either in society at large or by those who led the main political parties. It certainly never dominated the Conservative Party which, under Benjamin Disraeli, passed a wealth of legislation to improve working and living conditions, much of which was quite contrary to the ideology. Instead, it was based on an unrefined moral sense combined with a shrewd political fear of the possible consequences of continued laissez-faire. 'Classical' marketism has been a much more dominant strain in America, where the vast scale of unused resources and the ambition and acquisitiveness of an immigrant population have combined to give it a natural home.

The theoretical objections to such fundamentalism are numerous. Within economics it has been attacked at its base by a range of theories which have suggested that the 'free' markets on which it depends are impossible in some products and, even where possible, have an inbuilt tendency to degenerate into 'oligopolistic' markets, cartels or monopolies. The disruption and inefficiency caused by the 'trade cycle' are another flaw in the argument, one which led Keynes to map out a much larger economic role for the state. An even greater source of economic objections is the idea of 'externalities' or 'spillovers', those consequences of economic decisions which cannot be taken into consideration by market actors. These include environmental pollution and ugliness and social dislocation. Although it became fashionable to talk about these in the 1960s and 1970s, an awareness that the logic of the market can produce considerable consequences, which it cannot itself control or even consider, was demonstrated by many thinkers in the Victorian period. John Stuart Mill was certainly aware of such possibilities and the 'classical' economist Alfred Marshall was worried about the growth of London, concluding that a free market in land could not be permitted in a small and densely populated country like England.

In political theory market fundamentalism has been attacked since the mid-nineteenth century for its failure to recognise that the state is not the only agency which can, in realistic terms, coerce people and deprive them of their liberty. The activities of entrepreneurs and factory managers and the deprivations which result from mere callousness can restrain a person just as effectively as the state. These considerations (which once again John Stuart Mill articulated in the 1840s) led in electoral politics to the 'New Liberalism' which dominated the governments of 1906–14 and which stressed a 'positive' and 'liberating' role for the state in freeing people from ignorance, poverty and insecurity.

There are, of course, many other objections to market fundamentalism, often less precise than those discussed so far, but no less serious. The market, it can be said, takes no account of the realities of sociology, in the sense of the existence of groups and of power. People start the market game from vastly different positions in terms of resources; it would only make sense if they were roughly equal. However they cannot be made roughly equal, according to one account, without destroying the principles of acquisitiveness and inheritance which are necessary to the motives which make markets work. At a level which is even less precise, but even more important, many people would stress that the moral and psychological consequences of market society are unacceptable. The preoccupation with the self and with consumption, they say, can lead only to the 'shrink' and the suicide pill, an assertion not wholly contradicted by American experience. But a weaker, more moderate acceptance of the propriety and necessity of markets is a very vague thing altogether, amounting only to a belief that markets, in some sense, are the best available way of ordering some human activities. A proposition as vague as this would find few dissenters, and in the period of 'convergence' (from the mid–fifties to the mid–seventies) it did appear that the East was slowly rediscovering markets just as the West was slowly undermining them.

Since then there has been a move back to fundamentalism on both sides, especially by the believers in market individualism, who have advanced on several fronts. Von Hayek's arguments that all conditions other than the free market degenerate into 'serfdom' or 'feudalism' have become increasingly popular. Robert Nozick has revived a libertarian and individualist philosophy not unlike that of John Locke, from the very early stages of the 'modern' period. Edward Banfield has developed a sociological account of man in which aggregative phenomena such as class are understood in terms of the individuals' attitudes, especially the 'time horizons' within which they formulate their interests and make their plans, so that people in a market society get the class membership they deserve. Milton Friedman and other 'monetarists' have developed a theory of the state which reduces the proper role of public decisions to the control of the money supply.

This revival has taken place in the complete absence of any real rebuttal of the arguments against markets. Thus the 'New Right' have not returned to a complete faith in the market mechanism and its 'invisible hand'. What they have done is to argue that the market is the best available institution for many purposes and that it must be accepted on an all–or–nothing basis. We cannot pick and choose where to have markets as Keynesian and New Liberal exponents of the mixed economy suggest. If we do, we only succeed in encouraging the inexorable and insidious growth of the state at the expense of the market. It is reminiscent of Yeats' mysterious but graphic phrase, 'Things fall apart, the centre cannot hold.'

Marketism and conservatism are now virtually the same thing in America. The constitution, the intellectual heritage, the economic organisation and the self-image, the whole 'way of life' of the United States, clearly, and in ways which can be stated coherently, fit better on the intellectual platform of market individualism. Much more than any European society, America embodies an ideology. But the relation of marketism to conservatism in England is a great deal more complex. Its doctrines are much in favour with the Conservative Party at the time of writing, but they do not have the kind of widespread acceptance that they have in the United States and there are important beliefs which are, in England, recognisably conservative, which are in logical opposition to the main tenets of marketism.

The organic society

Many English conservatives would argue that marketism is anything but genuine conservatism. What, after all, does it promise to conserve? It is a radical doctrine, more dynamic and progressive than any form of socialism, not based on tradition, but on its opposite, a clear theory of what man is and how society should be organised. In seeking to explain the basis of conservatism they are likely to look at a tradition of treating society as an organic entity, a tradition most famously represented in the British Isles by Edmund Burke. In this tradition collective entities are not mere ways of talking about individuals. In extreme versions, such as the post-revolutionary writers Lammenais and De Maistre, there is even a denial that the individual can be said to exist at all outside of a specific social context.

Groups and classes may be important examples of the entities which give meaning and purpose to people's lives, but the most important are the nation and the family. Burke said that rights could only be said to belong to men as members of a nationality, not as men. De Maistre in his *Considerations on France* went further:

> The 1795 constitution, like its predecessors, was made for *man*. But there is no such thing as *man* in the world. During my life, I have seen Frenchmen, Italians, Russians and so on;

thanks to Montesquieu I know that one can be *Persian*; but I must say, as for *man*, I have never come across him anywhere; if he exists, he is completely unknown to me.

(Despite this, De Maistre is much more recognisable as a French equivalent of a Tory cosmologist and there are problems in reconciling his views on nationality with those on religion.)

The question of what makes a nation is complex. The simplest answer to emerge from nineteenth-century conservatism and nationalism is that language and the existence of a common heritage and consciousness which language creates are basic. But there are many examples which cannot be analysed in terms of language. In any case, much conservative writing in the organic tradition specifically argues that such questions as 'What is a nation?' cannot be answered with great precision. There is a kind of mysticism in the writings of Burke which insists that social relations are so complex that we cannot explain or understand them. Least of all can we restructure them on rational principles. A nation and its major political institutions develop in a slow and intricate manner, a thousand entities responding and developing in complex patterns to fit the whole. We must always take into account the possibility that we cannot remove the monarchy or institute an abstract doctrine of human rights without sending shattering vibrations throughout the system. Reform can therefore only be very gradual and partial, and must normally take place on the basis of restoring order and efficacity to the system by improving a malfunctioning part.

Thus there is a conservative view of politics which takes as its basis the importance of the organic nature of societies. The analogy of the organism has both positive and negative implications. Negatively, it stresses the complex interconnections between the parts of the organism and the consequent dangers and difficulties of radical change. This emphasis is very strong in the writings of Edmund Burke; because of the times in which he lived, he devoted a great deal of attention to the folly of trying to reconstruct societies according to the grand designs suggested by political theories.

But the analogy also suggests several attractions and advantages of life in a society which is not only like an organism but accepted and respected as being so. In an organic society the individual is part of something which has a character of its own beyond the complete control of conscious plans. His incorporation into this larger entity gives his life meaning, place and purpose. It makes him belong; it is the object of his capacity for loyalty; it offers motives and a focal point for his creativity. What is more, it has an existence which stretches from before recorded time into an indefinitely long future. 'In the long run we are all dead' said Lord Keynes, but there is no reason to suppose that our nation or our family cannot survive even the long term.

The 'organic' society can grow and change and modestly reform itself while remaining the same being; it has similarities to a living creature but it is not necessarily mortal. Part of its appeal is that it offers a highly attractive image of social life and this image fosters a conservatism which is patriotic and traditional as well as being cautious and gradualist. In many respects such conservatism is collectivist rather than individualist.

Pessimism and scepticism

It is legitimate in matters of ideas to be predominantly negative, to concentrate on revealing the flaws in the arguments of others. Much sound conservative argument concentrates on the weakness of the arguments for change rather than citing such grand conceptions as God's will or the organic nature of society. The negative arguments can be causal and pessimistic, concentrating on the improbability of change achieving its projected and desired effect. Here there is a series of mental entrenchments, which will be evident in the discussion of human nature and which can be used to oppose change. Or the arguments can be analytic and sceptical, concentrating on the incoherence and undesirability of the account of the projected effects of the proposed change. In my own view, this is the soundest plank of the conservative platform and the more specific arguments in this book will be in this style.

CONSERVATISM: CONTRADICTIONS AND DEFINITIONS

These elements of conservatism relate to each other in contradictory and confusing ways. To some extent they are completely opposites: much of the conservative tradition belittles any attempt to produce a theory of man and society, but market individualism, which is

now an important wing of conservatism, presents the most complete and refined (if narrow) theory of man on the intellectual menu.
To millions, religion and conservatism are inextricably linked, but
there is a long British tradition from Hume to Scruton, within
which I would wish to be included, which sees conservatism as the
only genuine emancipation from religion. Conservatives are indi-
vidualists and collectivists, authoritarians and freedom lovers,
mystics and sound practical men. . . .

In some ways, of course, these conflicting approaches reinforce
each other in practice. The Tory cosmology functions for much of
the time in the same way as a belief in the organic nature of society,
not least in that both encourage a reverence for the existing social
and political order. Scepticism and pessimism may discourage (re-
spectively) the theoretical belief in the interplay of human desire and
the idea that the free market is going to make men happier than they
have ever been before, but they are likely to prescribe extreme
caution with respect to any proposal to abolish market arrangements. Equally, the sceptic's distrust of absolute truth may lead him
to believe that the Tory cosmology is the best available belief for
most people: the most comforting, the least abrasive, the most
likely to lead them to act as if they had a sense of right and wrong.

But the contradictions are genuine and they cleave right down to
the base. Is there then (intellectually, as opposed to politically)
anything which can be called conservatism? Surprisingly, perhaps, I
think the answer is Yes in two senses, one formal and the other
substantive.

The formal sense is that, despite the contradictions, some reasonable covering definition of conservatism can be cobbled together. In
A Dictionary of Political Thought Roger Scruton calls conservatism
'The political outlook which springs from a desire to conserve
existing things, held to be either good in themselves, or better than
the likely alternatives, or at least safe, familiar and the objects of
trust and affection.' I would call it a state of mind in which the
relationship between attitudes to the present and past and attitudes
to possible futures generates a general tendency to protect present
institutions and to mistrust proposals for change.

'Attitudes' is a very vague term and both definitions are so
constructed as to cover a wide variety of positions. Attitudes include
beliefs (which have a truth value), but also principles and personal
preferences. It is, of course, possible to be conservative in quite

different ways. There is the way of the black pessimist, for instance, who may share radical values, but does not believe them to be attainable and believes that attempts to alter them can only lead to bloodshed and chaos. Conversely, the cheerful patriot may accept radical arguments, but not their values: a world of monarchs, peers, the Brigade of Guards and Rolls Royces may strike him as superior to anything else which is even claimed to be available. Or there is the true believer in Tory fairness who holds that the market and the hereditary principle are morally right and that socialism is wicked rather than foolish.

The more substantive way of explaining what conservatism is, is to explain in the most general terms what it is against. Broadly, conservatism is opposed to humanism, and the word 'humanism' has had a variety of meanings. In the sixteenth century it referred to those who believed that art and the intellectual life should be based on classical models; generally, being a humanist was considered compatible with Christian belief. In the twentieth century 'humanist' has often been used as a euphemism for 'atheist', but I am using it here in its broad and long-established sense as 'the religion of man'.

Humanism combines the following attitudes:

1 The belief in man as fundamentally superior to all other creatures (other than in his capacity for symbolic discourse).
2 Faith in man: the general precept that man is fundamentally 'good' or 'noble' and the particular propensity to trust other people.
3 The idea that man is necessarily moving towards some final state, that he has a 'destiny' or is making 'progress', typically toward some indefinitely durable form of society in which the tensions, problems and miseries of existing societies will be absent.
4 The assumption that men, as men, have common interests which can be cited to persuade them rationally to over-ride their divisions and differences.

Any one or more of these attitudes tends toward the mental condition of humanism. In other words humanism takes on many of the logical features of a religion, but contains no gods. It gives many of the properties possessed by gods in other religions to man.

Conservatism, for all its diversity and contradictions, is not human-ism; humanism, for all the variety of its forms, is not conservatism.

CONSERVATISM: MYTHS AND HALF TRUTHS

Many people would assume that conservatism is essentially a defence of capitalism. This is not true in England, though it is in the United States of America. It is difficult to imagine conservatives not favouring capitalism among the currently available alternative economic systems, but the American commentator Samuel Beer is surely right to suggest that English Toryism could survive the eclipse of capitalism. But it does, of course, depend on what is meant by 'capitalism'. In the fundamentalist sense, Beer is clearly right. There are weaker senses, though, in which 'capitalism' is used to describe any set of economic arrangements which has important elements of private ownership and market trading. In most of these senses capitalism is the normal condition of human society and it would be very odd for a conservative not to favour it.

Some people, like Robert Eccleshall, writing in *Political Studies*, have extended this approach to conservatism into the proposition that conservatism is an ideology for any ruling class. In a sense, this is true, but it is so trivial that it is misleading to bother saying it. It is a refusal to take the argument seriously, like saying that the essence of Christianity is that it is a device for keeping priests in secure employment. It is only a half-truth to say that conservatism is a pessimistic doctrine. As I have shown, there can be many ways of coming to the desire to oppose change which are not particularly pessimistic. In any case, 'pessimism' is systematically ambiguous: conservatism is a relation between what one believes about history as a whole and what one believes about one's own time and place: the latter must be optimistic in relation to the former if one is to be a conservative.

It is not very illuminating to say that conservatives want to conserve, because the perception and evaluation of what might be conserved can vary so enormously. Most humanists want to conserve something very ancient. As many commentators have pointed out, visions of anarchy or future communism normally incorporate some ancient goods: space, creativity, free association, social tranquillity and so on. Modern societies are frighteningly dynamic;

nothing can be preserved without something being destroyed. A detailed example: suppose we set out to preserve the character of an English village. We only allow a very limited amount of building and that must be in traditional materials. But that not only raises the cost of housing, it makes the housing market a sellers' market. Only well-off commuters and retired people can afford to buy houses in the village. The buildings remain, but the school, the cricket club, possibly even the pub, disappear from the village. In a constantly changing society, the more you try to preserve, the more you change.

So every conservative must be a conservative reformer. As they say in business management, 'the *status quo* is not an option.' Disraeli was a conservative reformer in a special sense: he aimed to incorporate those who were effectively excluded from society into a society which he considered had great merit. He wanted to incorporate them because they threatened society, but also because it was morally right to do so. But the more common condition of conservative reform is that of having to make complex and subtle judgements about both what can be preserved and what should. Conservatism is nothing if it is not subtle and flexible. It is even possible to be a conservative revolutionary if the *ancien régime* is bad enough and threatens existing practice and the revolutionaries are suitably modest about the transformation which they seek to make. Burke, after all, was sympathetic to the American revolution. Modern conservatives are necessarily utilitarians. Most of them, certainly Burke and even De Maistre, have committed themselves to the ultimate proposition that government exists to make its citizens happy and must be judged in relation to that end.

But it does become more difficult to know what being a conservative implies as one moves away from England, with its massive continuity of institutions and practices, and into other societies which are, to a greater or lesser extent, post-revolutionary. The most difficult problem for conservatives is: What do we do *after* the revolution? It would be easy to fall into misery and despair; Burke's later letters and essays reveal a very miserable old man, notwithstanding the fact that the British Isles had avoided revolution. Or absurdity, like De Maistre's claim that the French Republic did not really exist.

There are several solutions. One can work towards a formal and coercive restoration. Some conservatives accept the new regime, as

Hobbes transferred his allegiance to the Commonwealth and as millions of non-revolutionary Russians transferred theirs to Stalin. But the most logical reaction is to build on those social phenomena which can never quickly change: the family, the nation, trade and exchange, the long strands of cultural memory which link people to their past. And to attack, always, the overweening and overarching nonsense which lies at the foundation of humanism.

2

MAN

O Lord our Lord
How excellent is thy name in all the earth!
Who hast set thy Glory above the heavens.
Out of the mouth of babes and sucklings hast thou ordained
    strength
Because of thine enemies.
That thou mightest still the enemy and the avenger.
When I consider thy heavens, the work of thy fingers,
The moon and the stars, which thou has ordained;
What is man, that thou art mindful of him?
And the son of man, that thou visitest him?
For thou hast made him a little lower than the angels,
    and hast crowned him with glory and honour.
Thou madest him to have dominion over the works of thy
    hands;
Thou hast put all things under his feet:
All sheep and oxen,
Yea, and the beasts of the field;
The fowl of the air, and the fish of the sea,
And whatsoever passeth through the paths of the seas.
O Lord our Lord,
How excellent is thy name in all the earth!   (Psalm 8)

But the Bible offers another view of man, the two contrasting as
sharply as any two visions in modern literature:

    I said in mine heart concerning the estate of the sons of men,
that God might manifest them, and that they might see that

they themselves are beasts. For that which befalleth the sons of
men befalleth beasts; even one thing befalleth them: as the one
dieth, so dieth the other; yea, they have all one breath; so that a
man hath no preeminence over a beast: for all is vanity. All go
unto one place; all are of the dust, and all turn to dust again.
(Ecclesiastes 3, 18–20)

My purpose in quoting these passages is not connected with
problems of theology or textual analysis (whether, for instance, the
preacher king really meant it), but merely to illustrate the age and
profundity of the divisions between men's views of man. The three
plural nouns: men, humans, persons and the three abstract nouns:
mankind, humanity, the human race: I shall assume they label the
same concept. The plural nouns refer to the individuals and the
abstract expressions to a concept which applies only to those individuals.

It is an important concept, fundamental to political theory. The
attribution, for instance, of rights or equality to human beings has
no sense unless we know what human beings are. In its broadest
sense, political theory has often been seen as the study of human
nature. But the question 'What is man . . .?' contains at least two
questions. The first of these is a conceptual question, being the
analytic question 'What makes a thing a man?' The second question
is contingent, but with vast philosophical overtones and complica-
tions. It is the synthetic question, 'What is man like . . . essentially,
immutably?' In principle, we should look to language for the answer
to the first question and to the world for an answer to the second.

THE CONCEPT OF MAN

'Human', 'man' etc. seem to be relatively straightforward concepts.
It is far easier to tell a human from a non-human than it is to tell a
bourgeois from a proletarian, a rational actor from one who is
irrational or a sane person from a lunatic. We make distinctions
between human and non-human entities all the time and our per-
centage of error is very small. Yet the concept easily generates
paradox. If we found a skeleton or a foetus we might want to know
whether it was human. We could ask an expert to find out and he

could tell us (more or less) for certain. But to describe a skeleton as a human being would be wrong and to describe a foetus as a human being would be highly controversial.

Clearly, there are at least two senses of human (*et al*). In one of those senses the terms are entirely co-extensive with the biological (and essentially straightforward) concept of *homo sapiens*. But we also talk about human beings in a way which goes beyond mere biological classification. People exist in an extra dimension from animals and things. In this case, at least, the analogy of a dimension is precise: just as there is a fundamental difference between the ways in which we can talk about a three-dimensional object as compared with one of two dimensions, so the range of concepts applying to humans is much greater than that applying to non-humans. People can be talked of in non-human ways (as physical objects and as animals) just as three-dimensional entities can be described from one aspect as if they were two-dimensional. In both cases, the more restricted form of talk can be both truthful and useful, but is necessarily limited and potentially misleading.

What is the extra dimension which makes us human? Alternatively, what are they? For there may be more than one. There are plenty of claimants which can easily be rejected on the grounds that they do not make the distinction we seek. Men are not uniquely tool-using; a creature as relatively lowly (in nineteenth-century terms) as a thrush uses tools. Humans are not alone in controlling their environment: that is, there is no precise distinction between the ways in which people do it and those in which beavers and, for that matter, most birds do. It is arbitrary to say that man is uniquely artistic; much birdsong and many mating calls are difficult to distinguish from human art, and monkeys have produced marketable paintings.

Least of all are men uniquely 'rational'. In the precise sense in which economists use the term which distinguishes beings which have order and pursue objectives from those which haven't or don't, many non-humans behave as if they were rational to a greater degree than humans. There appears to be far greater clarity of purpose in the beehive than in the city. There are broader definitions of rationality, but these are of little help. Indeed, in terms of at least one of the conditions of rationality which John Rawls stipulates in his *A Theory of Justice* ('the bare knowledge of the difference between their condition and that of others is not, within certain limits and in ing is in them and we know what sort of things – beliefs, values,

itself, a source of great dissatisfaction'), much human behaviour is markedly less rational than most bird behaviour.

The serious candidates for the name of man's unique dimension are: the soul, the mind, reason, self-consciousness. These are the names of the distinctions which have been made between men and other entities throughout the mainstream of intellectual history. But what kinds of concepts are they? Without prior knowledge or assumption of divine endowment nothing can demonstrate that rabbits lack souls. Many thousands of species of creature have brains, which differ only in degree from those of *homo sapiens*. Many mammals make complex strategic decisions, whereas 'error' is regarded as typically human. The navigation of the pigeon, the construction of the beaver, the food selection capacity of the blue tit and the maze-cracking abilities of the brown rat represent successful solutions to complex problems; some of them also demonstrate a capacity to learn and to reapply techniques. To dismiss these as forms of 'instinct' while elevating what goes on in a supermarket, a discotheque or a sociology conference as something incomparably 'higher' seems arbitrary, groundless and boastful.

Only one thing allows us to claim that we are uniquely self-conscious: we can talk to each other and such talk leads each to assume that the other is thinking. In other words, all considerations of 'soul', 'reason' and so on *without God* can be reduced to a distinction of language. The crucial distinction is not between creatures which have language and those which do not, because an enormous variety of species possess systems of communication which signal, for instance, fear, attraction and hostility. But the capacities for forming concepts and making propositions do distinguish men, at least from the overwhelming majority of other creatures. We know that other human beings have 'minds' because they can tell us what is in them and we know what sort of things – beliefs, values, principles, and so on – constitute a mind (as opposed to a mere brain) because we have a propositional and concept-forming language.

All the special intellectual properties of man collapse, upon examination, into a distinction concerning the structure of communication. Otherwise, cats have a 'moral sense', because they appear to act guiltily. Human love and loyalty rarely approach the level of Greyfriars Bobby. If either of these qualities – love and duty – are really on different levels in *homo sapiens* than in the meticulous and monogamous mute swan, it is only because they have a proposional dimension. Rabbits, in *Watership Down*, have dreams and visions and tell legends. Real rabbits may have dreams and visions, but we cannot know of them. It is vastly improbable that they have legends because the overwhelming, if circumstantial, evidence is that they have no propositional capacity.

TWO CONCEPTS OF MAN

So far, we have come across two answers to the analytic form of the question 'What is man?' The first says 'Man equals *homo sapiens*. Ask a biologist, if you have doubts about something you have found in your garden.' The second says, 'Man is the thinking, or propositional, creature. Anything you can talk to – even in principle – is human.'

The two answers are wholly logically independent. The *sapiens* of *homo sapiens* does not stipulate or imply propositional capacity, and even if it did, there is nothing in the orthodox taxonomy which precludes the possibility of (say) *rattus sapiens*. Though logically independent, the two concepts are more or less co-extensive on this planet: pretty well everything that speaks is a *homo sapiens* and pretty well every *homo sapiens* has some capacity for speech. The co-extension is not total, though. There are certainly some members of *homo sapiens* who lack propositional capacity; these may include the dramatic examples of wolf-boy and gazelle-boy, and they do include the more mundane cases of those who are drastically mentally handicapped. There may also be non-*homo sapiens* creatures who can just about stagger across the frontier into symbolic and representative communication. This could include chimpanzees (depending on the interpretation of the 'Nevada experiment') and possibly dolphins, but there are no clear and agreed concept-formers and symbol-users apart from *homo sapiens*.

Despite these exceptions, the degree of co-extension between the two concepts of man is very large, so much so that most people could (and probably do) live their lives in ignorance of the exceptions and on the assumption that the meaning of 'man' was single and obvious. On the contrary, that we are able to talk about 'men' as we do is, ignoring religious explanations, a pure coincidence.

There is no logical reason why there should not be other self-conscious creatures on earth; that one species appears to have a monopoly of propositional communication is a massive and mere contingency. The discovery of Australia led to the discovery of creatures which were properly described as swans, but which were black. This emphasised that 'swans are white' is contingent and false. It is also merely contingent that there were, and are, no philosophising kangaroos in Australia. If there were it would be equally clear that 'human beings are featherless bi-peds' is contingent and may yet be false. If we meet space travellers from another planet and are able to exchange information, ideas and theories with them, we will be treating them as essentially human, whatever their shape and size.

Representative thought is a necessary condition of being human. Consider other mammals. Rabbits are *sentient*: they experience, they perceive, they have emotions. That is, they manifest the physical dimensions (both behaviourally and neurologically) of fear, pleasure etc. The distinction between us and them lies not in the range of reactions but in the dimensions in which those reactions exist. But representative thought is not sufficient to establish humanness. Humans must also be sentient. A computerised humanoid robot would be difficult to accept as human, even if it were very sophisticated and programmed to react emotionally. An anger-and-distress response stimulated by any reference to the Soviet Union would remain different in kind from the genuine emotion which we and the rabbits experience.

The account of man in Psalm 8 has considerable advantages. For those who can believe that there is a creator of the universe whose intentions uniquely determine right and wrong, the information that he has given *homo sapiens* a special status and complete dominion over other creatures aids both the theoretical aspects of morality and social organisation and the practical necessities of hunting and farming. It is worth remembering, though, that Psalm 8 was written in the context of two other assumptions: that God created the universe in six days and that he chose a race as well as a species. Insofar as the credibility of the Psalm 8 account is dependent on the status of the Bible as revealed truth, the reader cannot pick and choose; the authoritative nature of the source can only be maintained if it is all accepted. Without biblical revelation the assertion that *homo sapiens* is different in kind from other species and uniquely and universally worthy of consideration lacks anything which can be taken seriously as a moral argument. It is biological chauvinism, a mere speciesism morally equivalent to racism. It says only that 'featherless bipeds rule OK.'

It seems equally inappropriate to regard propositional capacity as an adequate basis for constructing man's status and worth. As Bentham stressed in the *Deontology*, feeling and sentience seem a reasonable basis for the most important of moral distinctions, which is the distinction of those creatures worthy of consideration from those not so worthy. Talk seems wholly irrelevant. That pain should be avoided and pleasure created can plausibly claim to be a serious moral principle. In the absence of a directive from God, the stipulation that talking creatures should be afforded a universal and unique respect is groundless and arbitrary. Thus, there is a major conceptual problem for humanism: that our habitual way of talking about humanity depends on a mere coincidence and cannot be translated into anything which is both coherent and morally serious.

THE SYNTHETIC PROBLEM: WHAT IS MAN LIKE?

Many of the most famous accounts of mankind stress that the state of being human is, not by definition, but in reality, a state of tension. A century and more before Darwin raised debates about apes and angels, Pope described man as:

Plac'd on this isthmus of a middle state,
A being darkly wise and rudely great:
With too much knowledge for the Sceptic side,
With too much weakness for the Stoic's pride.
He hangs between; in doubt to act, or rest,
In doubt to deem himself a God, or Beast;
In doubt his Mind or Body to prefer
Born but to die, and reas'ning but to err

. . .

But when his own great work is but begun,
What Reason weaves, by Passion is undone.

More recently, in *A Distant Mirror*, Barbara Tuckman has seen the tension at the centre of human existence as well exemplified by medieval chivalry:

[Knights] were supposed, in theory, to serve as defenders of
the Faith, upholders of justice, champions of the oppressed. In
practice, they were themselves the oppressors, and by the 14th
century the violence and lawlessness of men of the sword had
become a major agency of disorder. When the gap between
ideal and real becomes too wide, the system breaks down.
Legend and story have always reflected this; in the Arthurian
romances the Round Table is shattered from within. The
sword is returned to the lake: the effort begins anew. Violent,
destructive, greedy, fallible as he may be, man retains his
vision of order and resumes his search.

In political philosophy, but also in daily political debate, much
appears to rest on the relationship between love and hate, order and
violence, community and egoism. What is immutable and what
contingent? Much of what deeply divides 'left' from 'right' in the
modern world seems located in this area. It is recognisably 'right-
wing' to regard lust, acquisitiveness, ambition, jealousy, malice,
mistrust and violence as typically and immutably human. Thus
order can only be achieved through coercive law, systems of status,
hierarchies of office and regulated markets in goods and services. In
this aspect conservatism is typified, to use Anthony Quinton's
phrase, as *The Politics of Imperfection*. Conversely, it is typically 'left-
wing' to explain known and existing imperfections in terms of
contingent sociology. At the broad level, idealists must believe in
the possibility of the state 'withering away' as Marx expects, or
being abolished, as many anarchists recommend. But the differences of vision can be revealed in the particular discussion of a
single riot. It can be understood in terms of poor policing, an
inadequate system of punishment, the decline of religion or a failure
of parental discipline. These would be typically 'right-wing'
emphases. To emphasise social injustice, class tension or the failures
of the economic system would be equally recognisable as a 'left-
wing' view.

   Thus sometimes and to some extent the difference between conservatives and 'radicals' is, at its core, the difference between pessi-
mists and idealists. The position has to be expressed in this guarded
and qualified way. After all, Disraeli was both a conservative and an
intellectual, but when he considered the two visions of man he was
'in favour of the angels'. I have often thought that he was wrong to

be so, a man who was practical and literary rather than philosophical. But conservative pessimism does not depend on a black vision of man. To establish the institutional consequences of pessimism man does not have to be portrayed as universally or essentially bad, only partially and immutably so. 'Pessimism' and 'optimism' are not symmetrical in this respect. The pessimist can believe that man is as good as he is bad, if not more so, but the optimist must believe that man is essentially, transcendentally or naturally good and only contingently bad if he is to write off as contingent the historical record of man.

The historical record is highly consistent and favours pessimism. Kropotkin insisted that in essence man was a 'social animal', but freely conceded that in the reality of history so far, 'Man is the cruellest animal upon earth.'

The behaviour of man shows great consistency, especially between societies with high levels of complexity and sophistication. Reading Suetonius on the *Twelve Caesars* is unmistakably reminiscent of reading the *News of the World*, not only because of the tales of lust, malice and ambition which both contain, but also because of the combination of censoriousness and nudging delight which both convey. W. J. M. Mackenzie, as a classical scholar removed to Whitehall during the second world war and set to study the relations between the British government and various European resistance movements, found that 'there was nothing there that was not in Thucydides' history of the Peloponnesian war in the fifth century BC.' In the eighteenth century, Hume described politics thus: 'The face of the earth is continually changing, by the encrease of small kingdoms into great empires, by the dissolution of great empires into smaller kingdoms, by the planting of colonies, by the migration of tribes. Is there anything discoverable in all these events but force and violence?' Hume's answer, of course, is No. His may be a limited view of history, but it is no more and no less supportable in the late twentieth century than when he wrote.

DOES HISTORY PROVE ANYTHING?

Conservatives ought, perhaps, to insist that children should be made to study history in great detail. History shows how vast is the range of dark possibilities which man faces. It shows, for instance, that anything which could claim to be a free and equal society has been of short duration, often degenerating into the lynch mob or the bitter schism or falling victim to the 'charismatic' leader or the outside massacre. A casual reading of history suggests that trust is appropriate only in very limited and specific circumstances. Violence and force will always be necessary, if only to restrain violence and force. Hierarchy, authority and coercion are necessary if there are to be 'arts, letters and society' as Hobbes put it.

But what is such a casual reading of history worth? In itself it is just a collection of selective observations and intuitive judgements. Treated in this way, without theory, history is like news, just one dreary, squalid event after another. Furthermore, history is very, very, short. Compare it with other scales of time: 2,000 million years of 'life'; ten million years of hominids; 100,000 years of man, but a tiny handful of millenia of 'history'. That so much happened in such a short time is due to man's very special qualities of adaptivity, his generalised capacity for choosing what survival requires and thus being able to survive in a far wider range of environments than most other creatures. It is this capacity which has led Robert Ardrey to label man 'the bad-weather animal'. To understand exactly what is special about man we must distinguish between three ways in which animals change.

1   Adaptation. In the 'Darwinian' sense that creatures 'evolve', that is they develop and respond to changes in their environment (among which changes in climate are the most basic and important), 'adaptation' is a highly misleading expression, because no act of adapting takes place. All that happens is that mutations occur which have different probabilities of survival in an environment which may vary from near constancy to dramatic change.

2   Adaptability. Many creatures learn (and teach) responses to a changing environment. A local example (for an Englishman) is the capacity of blue tits to steal milk from bottles on doorsteps, a practice which was, at one time, widespread in some areas, but non-existent in others. The responses of many domestic creatures to their masters' needs and whims can be considered as adaptability, most clearly when practices are taught by other creatures as happens (for instance) among sheepdogs.

3 Adaptivity. This is the uniquely 'general purpose' capacity
of man to adapt to changing circumstances. Whereas man's
adaptivity makes him flexible to a vastly different degree
than other creatures, this only requires a different concept
insofar as man uses a propositional language to make tech-
nological gains. Of course, the two phenomena have a
spiralling relationship: man developed language because of
his superior capacity to adapt and his capacity to adapt is
much enhanced by his possessing a propositional language.

But whether or not it reduces to another concept or a matter of
degree, it is undeniable that the range of change and self-reform
which man might achieve, in principle at least, could be on an
entirely different scale from such change as we have seen so far.
Thus history is of little relevance to man's potential: it is short and
dynamic; it may even be accelerating.

Moreover history, as an account of man's viciousness, can be
analysed sociologically. Kropotkin, a biologist, saw nothing in the
biology of man which required him to be cruel. Social institutions
mould man into cruelty: the state, property, authority, the law.
When these are destroyed (necessarily by revolution), man's potential can be released. Marxism adds a developmental dimension to
anarchism, and one in apparent sympathy with the natural history
of man and the implications of adaptivity, so that man's nature can
be seen as a systematically changing context of social and economic relations. In other words, history demonstrates nothing determinate about human nature: if we are looking for proof, it will have
to be sought at the level of biology rather than history.

GENETICS AND POLITICS

Kropotkin may not have been able to discover any biological evidence to support pessimism about man's nature, but the vast
advances in bio-chemistry since his time tell a different story. The
greatest of these advances is the investigation of the gene, the single
great programming, motivating piece of chemistry which is the key
to understanding individual development. The gene, as Richard
Dawkins put it, is 'selfish', its only direction, and one which it

pursues fiercely, being self-perpetuation. So far as contemporary science is concerned, man is not programmed to concern himself with the survival, still less the improvement, of the species, not even the survival of the person, but with the perpetuation of the gene. In vulgar terms, what modern science says about man's nature is that he is tough, nasty and highly sexed.

The idea that man is a 'social animal', as Kropotkin put it, is extraordinarily weak. Man is by no means the most social of creatures: he is one of the most unsocial, the most individual, the least dependent on cooperation. The weak sense in which he is 'social' does not preclude a very strong sense in which he can be said to be 'anti-social'. Genetics tells us that there are severe limits to man's sociability.

Sexuality is perhaps the key to understanding sociability. It is the human expression of physical genetics. It brings us together, but draws us apart into jealousies, rivalries and family loyalties. More clearly than any other aspect of our being it suggests a chink of darkness, an ineradicable doubt about man's affinity to the angels. William Morris's *News from Nowhere* is set in a society in which law, money, property and the state have vanished, taking with them almost all violence and social tension. But only almost, because in Morris's vision of future communism one source of tension, violence and even murder remains: jealousy.

Even relatively 'hard' scientific analysis of man proves nothing about human nature, at the level at which philosophers discuss it. Understanding the gene does not remove the tension between man's motivations and his principles. A belief in egalitarian socialism is as 'real' as is lust. Dawkins is very quick to insist that the biologist cannot bridge the fact/value gap. Genetics give us no social values; nor would the discovery of ineradicable differences between the brains of different races give us a principle for race relations. It is arguably right (and even part of man's essence) that man should fight against his genetic nature. This struggle might be carrried into the field of genetic engineering, a possibility opened by man's apparently limitless adaptivity. Genetic engineering in the interests of social harmony would be very complex and some would consider it distasteful, but it is possible in principle and an idealist might coherently recommend it.

THE RETREAT TO RATIONALITY

Neither history nor biology proves anything about human nature
in the sense in which it has been philosophically contended. The
best move for the pessimist who is trying to establish his case on as
firm a basis as possible would seem to be that he move away from
proof toward an insistence on a rational evaluation of the available
arguments.

After all, a pessimistic view of human nature and of the possibilities of social improvement depends only on minimal premises. It
certainly does not require any assumption that men are universally,
nor even predominantly, wicked. It only requires that an element of
wickedness should be present in all social circumstances above a
minimal level of complexity. The argument from corruption will
do the rest. All the bad qualities of man have the potential to
corrupt: the headmasterly metaphor of the one rotten apple ruining
the barrel is accurate and even mathematically demonstrable. Malice
breeds malice. Selfishness puts enormous pressure on altruism.
Imagine a communal society of hard-working, unselfish people,
self-disciplined and cooperative. Then introduce into it one clever,
idle, lustful and domineering cynic. . . . Or a world which consisted
of 150 societies of pacific, contented libertarians and one state which
was nationalistic, militaristic and ideological. . . .

The pessimist's rational appeal would say, in essence: 'Look at the
historical record of man. Compare it with the biological science of
man. Consider the nature of corruption. Then ask yourself whether
a rational man, faced with a choice of assumptions about matters
which are not susceptible to proof, could avoid making pessimistic
assumptions about the potential for human and social improvement.'

But even this does not work. Unless rationality is extended from
the capacity to formulate and order preferences to include certain
preferences, then pessimism does not follow from rationality. In
particular, the argument requires assumptions about risk-aversion
and the time-horizon of considerations. Conservatives are likely to
be averse to risk and to have relatively short time horizons. If they
meet a man who is off to fight for socialism, they might tell him that
he is highly unlikely to achieve anything and that he is probably

only going to cause suffering for himself and others. But he is entitled to reply that the suffering is trivial in the context that matters and that any chance of achieving socialism is worth seizing.

It can still be claimed quite properly that the preferences of the pessimist are normal and widely shared and even that they are uniquely sensible or reasonable approaches to social alternatives. But these are theoretically weak terms; they may be useful in practical politics, but they depend on judgements. There are several counter-claims which an optimist can make. Faith, he might say, is morally and spiritually superior to lack of faith. Equally, in a world of uncertainty, hope is vastly preferable to hopelessness. Perhaps even more important is the centrality of the Mertonian idea of self-fulfilling prophecy in social understanding. Self-fulfilment pervades social relations; beliefs cannot be held in detachment from reality. Belief that men are brutes leads to treating them as brutes which turns them into brutes.

CONCLUSIONS

Perhaps pessimism has been over-stated as a central plank of conservatism. It is possible only to establish that in many cases most people's preferences are likely to be such that a mistrustful view of humanity and a cautious approach to social reform will represent the rational choice of assumptions. But even this excludes only the fanatics and millenarians, the likes of Morris and Kropotkin. It is no argument against liberals or reformers nor even those revolutionaries (including Marx in many moods) who stress that the road to paradise is long and hard and that we may require a brutal determination to reach the destination.

Conservatives should not answer the groundless and dangerous faith of the idealist simply with its opposite. Rather they should rely on judgement to make practical decisions and on conceptual scepticism for a theoretical basis. By conceptual scepticism I mean a philosophic doubt not about whether ideals can be achieved, but about whether they actually mean anything, at least anything that could be taken seriously as a goal. In the early section of this chapter I expressed doubts about whether 'humanity' meant anything that could be morally serious. In the same way, later chapters will doubt equality, justice and rights.

3

CONCEPTS AND
THEORIES

'Debates on political matters have happened for centuries' the
guide said when showing tourists the Houses of Parliament.
'Anything settled yet?' a voice said from the rear.
Reverse side of matchbox, England's Glory,
by Bryant and May Ltd

Anybody who is paid to study and teach politics must be acutely
aware of the embarrassment of having to answer the question 'What
do you do?' Academic lawyers, doctors and engineers must positively look forward to being asked the question: everybody thinks
they understand what they do and (in two of the three cases) how
useful they are and what kinds of progress have been made in their
subjects. Physicists, chemists, biologists and so on can at least treat
the question with equanimity: as natural scientists they will be
respected for their specialist knowledge. History and the arts have
long careers as important parts of the educational system. Linguists
have their uses. The importance (though perhaps not the usefulness)
of economics is obvious. Even sociology seems to be going somewhere.

Anyone who studies and teaches politics lacks these advantages.
He even lacks a name for his trade: 'politician' is certainly not right
and 'political scientist', though widely used in the United States, is
considered pretentious and misleading in England. He cannot
answer any of the commonest questions about his subject: 'Who
will win the next election?' 'Who can get us out of this mess?' 'Who
really has the power in this country?' 'What *is* politics?' All are

beyond him; that is, he may have clear and articulate answers to these questions, but he cannot speak with the authority of his subject, nor simply report what *is* the case. There is no obvious use for his subject. Its most spectacular failing is its lack of progress. In comparison, most academic subjects seem fairly new *and* to be making progress. As a subject, politics is very old, but is still failing to answer questions which troubled Plato and Socrates 24 centuries ago.

Some of the difficulties of politics as a subject are the difficulties of studying human beings. These are shared with other subjects and will be discussed at some length later in this book. But others seem to lie in the nature of the *concepts* which compose the subject: the state, politics, sovereignty, power, democracy, rights, law, interests. All of them react like the intellectual equivalents of pieces of wet soap; they are slippery, difficult to grasp. No sooner have you worked out a neat, watertight definition of what 'the state' is, and you are about to make some pertinent observations about the function and limits of the state, than along comes a critic who says that you are not really talking about the state at all and that you have ignored either the central point or an entire dimension of the state's existence.

It is well worth considering the recent history of the concept of power. There are two reasons for this: 'power' is a typical political concept and it has been considered by many people to be central to political discourse. In 1935 the concept's future as the central concept of politics seemed assured It was a 'hard-nosed', objective quality which many of the concepts which had absorbed previous generations (like sovereignty and citizenship) lacked. It was a concept well in spirit with a secular and scientific age: sceptical, realistic, objective, potentially quantifiable. Bertrand Russell, in his book, *Power: a new social analysis*, argued that power was the central concept in the study of society in exactly the same way that energy was the central concept in physics. Politicians, journalists and academics went on record in their hundreds saying that 'Politics is about power.' The future of the concept as the core of the study of politics seemed assured, as did the future of the subject as the study of power.

It was orthodox to believe two generalisations about power: that in most if not all states it was highly concentrated and that the concentration was becoming more intense. The former conclusion owed something to the 'classical' elite sociology of Gaetano Mosca,

Vilfredo Pareto and Robert Michels, but even more to a context in which Hitler, Stalin and Mussolini figured prominently. The latter owed something to the fears of liberals, like Russell, of the growing frontiers of the state and was to evolve the concept of 'totalitarianism' which became briefly central to the study of politics. This was given enormous emotional force and popular appeal by such novels as George Orwell's *1984* which dramatised the concept of totalitarianism into a nightmare. Orwell's vision owed much to Russell's theory (Orwell had reviewed Russell's book in the magazine *New Adelphi*), so much so that the interrogator O'Brian in *1984* repeats passages from *Power* almost verbatim. Further evidence of the importance and concentration of power came from some of the first 'empirical' work on the subject, conducted by Floyd Hunter in Atlanta, Georgia, and published in 1953. Hunter used a 'reputational' method: he asked people who had power over them and found that their answers consisted of a small circle of people.

It was at this point (roughly the mid-1950s) that the issue of power became very contentious. Many American academics, among whom Robert Dahl was the most prominent, felt that two things were wrong with work like Hunter's. First, it seemed to reduce the very complex reality of American politics, upon which many actors appeared to have an impact, to a simple and exclusive structure. Second, there was more than a suspicion that the 'reputational' method would turn up a 'power elite' however politics really worked: quite simply, there are very few people of whom most people have heard. So Dahl and others conducted 'well defined' empirical observations in which they isolated 'key' issues and recorded who was able to get their own way.

This produced a very different picture of the power structure. Many people were shown to exercise an influence on the decisions of city government: channels of influence and communication stretched to virtually all the citizens through such organisations as precinct parties, unions and parent-teacher associations. Even those who were clearly important in making decisions had only a limited, 'situational' power over a narrow range of issues. Far from being a pyramid-shaped power structure, the political system was 'pluralist', a 'polyarchy'.

The supporters of the elite model responded with new and powerful arguments. Peter Bachrach became the most prominent figure in this attack. The flaw in Dahl's method, went their argument, lies in the notions of an 'issue' and a 'key' issue. What makes something a political issue? Precisely that it is something the elite disagree about. Take the question of whether or not the means of production should be privately owned, a question on which the interests of the elite and the non-elite sharply conflict. This, of course, is not an issue on the political agenda in America: it has been educated, propagandised and manipulated out of the political system. The power of the powerful is not to be seen in their winning political 'issues'; it is to be seen in their ability to define what counts as an issue at all. For Bachrach and his allies 'non-decisions' were the key to power. Bachrach talked about a 'second face' of power, far more important than the first face, the ability to win overt political battles. Steven Lukes later extended this to three 'dimensions'. It turned out that this was the understanding of power which Antonio Gramsci had been developing since before Russell wrote. But he was writing in Italian and in prison and was a communist, so it took a long time before he had much impact on the English-speaking world.

The counter-counter-attack usually concentrated on the concept of interests. Clearly those who believed in the elite model had an idea of what was in people's interests which was not equivalent to, nor even reducible to, what those people felt that they wanted. The American people were actually in favour of capitalism – liked it, approved of it. It was arbitrary and dangerous to say that it was not in their interests and that their beliefs and attitudes were the consequence of power exercised over them. Such treatment of 'power' was not well-defined, but merely ideological.

By the 1970s it was clear that the issue was not going to be resolved. It was observed by all sides that 'empirical' work was actually a fake, its conclusions being contained in, and predestined by, its definitions and assumptions. Furthermore, the whole issue was not a methodological dispute between scientists, but another form of the ideological squabble between left and right. Distinguished figures like James March and W. J. M. Mackenzie concluded that studying power was futile. Others, mainly on the 'left', persisted, accepting the ideological nature of the debate and producing 'committed' analyses of power, like Steven Lukes' 'radical' view. These tended to merge with some rather mystical ideas about power emanating from sociology; in these terms power 'inhered' in social structures – it could not be measured, observed or isolated from its context and it was not possible to identify the individuals who possessed it.

Perhaps it is misleading to say that power is a 'typical' political concept; there is no such thing. It is typical of a particular approach to politics which reached the peak of its popularity in the middle of the twentieth century. Many political concepts present a problem which is not immediately presented by the concept of power: they have favourable or unfavourable connotations. The extreme example in modern political argument is 'democracy' which, since 1945, has had such a universally favourable connotation that argument about democracy has tended to become competition for the use of the word 'democracy'.

It is already clear, without giving any thought to the nature of science, that 'power' is not like 'energy'. When physicists talk about energy, even when they argue, there is an important sense in which they know and agree what they are talking about. Energy is a concept which is used to explain physical events, within certain rules of explanation. But academic students of politics may not know or agree what they are talking about when they discuss power: they may differ on assumptions, purposes and definitions. To some, power must exist, to others it may. For some the purpose is to provide a 'critical' acount of society, while others aspire to produce an 'objective' account.

To understand the problems of political concepts, one cannot avoid the question of what concepts are. They are not mere words, or at least not quite. 'Cricket' is not a concept: the word cricket covers an important game and a trivial insect. There might be a concept of the game of cricket. A concept is a word taken in conjunction with the rules and conventions governing its use. We can distinguish when somebody has a certain concept (when he has 'mastered' or 'grasped' it) and when he hasn't. There are at least two levels in the mastery of a concept. In the case of the concept of a 'bird' these are, first, being able consistently to distinguish between birds and other entities and, second, being able to say what makes a thing a bird.

'Concepts' come in three main kinds which can be called 'the straightforward, the failed and the contentious.' Straightforward concepts are those which have clear rules and conventions governing their application, so that we can say of any use or definition of the word which serves as the label of the concept, 'correct' or 'incorrect'.

There are two sources of our information in these respects. The first is 'ordinary' or 'natural' language and dealing with concepts in this respect consists of observing and extrapolating from the ways in which people use words. 'That isn't a house' means 'that isn't what people would call a house.' Linguistic philosophy, in its strongest form, insists that many important philosophical problems can be solved by reference to the underlying rules of ordinary language. J. L. Austin provided solutions to the philosophical problems of knowledge, truth, reality and responsibility by reference to the normal usage of words like 'know', 'false', 'see' and 'deliberately'.

Even if one finds Austin's argument convincing (and I do, to a considerable extent), there remain many problems which ordinary language does not solve. This is particularly true in politics, where there are few established and routinely understood conventions governing the use of important words. It may well be worth listening to Hodge in the public bar to find out what the difference between a real tractor and an imaginary one is or what counts as 'knowing' something. But it will not tell us what democracy is; what Hodge says in this area will be dependent not only on the level of his interest in and knowledge about politics, but also on which political party he supports.

A more fruitful source, statistically, of information about straightforward concepts is authority. By this I mean books (including dictionaries), established sources and persons which define expertise. The vast majority of words which fill the (unabridged) dictionaries are of this sort, words with precise rules for application which are not commonly known. The largest group of these are the categories of biology. Few people know what makes a bird a sedge warbler, but there are determinate answers to definitional questions about sedge warblers. Common sense might tell us that a dolphin is a fish, or a slow worm is a snake, but an authoritative orthodoxy tells us that the dolphin is a mammal and the slow worm is a legless lizard. We accept the authority before we know or accept its propositions. Authoritative sources do exist in politics, but they are detailed and peripheral. Experts can tell you what counts as a single transferable vote system or a filibuster. But they cannot tell you, at least not with the same authority, what the difference is between a right and a privilege.

At the other end of the spectrum from straightforward concepts are failed concepts, what W. B. Gallie calls 'radically confused' concepts. These are the labels which cannot usefully be used because there are no rules and conventions to compose a well-formed concept. There are many religious, political and aesthetic concepts in current usage which I believe are radically confused, but as examples they would be highly controversial. Uncontroversial examples can only be found outside current usage in the dustbin of history: phlogiston, ether and the *élan vital*, for instance.

There remain, in the middle, the contentious concepts, those which, while not being straightforward, do appear to mean something. Typically, they have changed meaning, there are arguments about their meaning and those arguments become mixed both with disputes about facts and with conflicts of values. These are the terms which Gallie has labelled 'essentially contested concepts' and politics is full of them: rights, liberty, interests, power, democracy, justice, equality and so on. Straightforward concepts generate 'brute' facts, as some philosophers call them: undeniable observations expressed in precise and well-established terms. Political concepts generate 'essential contest', complex dispute on shifting ground.

The concept of a concept presents a paradox. Those words and phrases which most clearly label concepts such as 'sedge warbler', 'cheese', 'carburettor' and 'Justice of the Peace' are not thought of as concepts, but as things, because they present no problems. Conversely, those words which may not label a concept at all, such as beauty, God and justice, which remain mere areas of debate, noises with associated ideas, are those which we think of as concepts and include in university courses on 'key concepts in . . .'. When is a concept not a concept? When it's officially recognised as a concept in a university course.

THE TRICKS OF POLITICAL LANGUAGE

Politics lacks a technical language, a set of purpose-built concepts for taking academic discussion away from the emotions and ambiguities of ordinary language. Much political language is emotive, in the sense that the American philosopher C. L. Stevenson used in constructing his 'emotive theory of ethical terms'. Stevenson distinguished two kinds of meanings which words have. 'Descriptive' meanings suggest rules and conventions for the application of terms, well established and not depending in any way on the attitude of the user. Dynamic meanings express an attitude: they evaluate and prescribe. Thus 'cylinder' is entirely descriptive in meaning while 'good' is entirely dynamic. These properties are not, of course, in the sounds or the symbols themselves, but in the conventions governing their use. The conventions could change, either over time or within a particular sub-culture, so that the cult insult might be, 'You're a cylinder, that's what you are, sunshine', while people might be heard saying 'This beer is good in the technical sense of the word, being alive and unpressurised.'

Many words have both dynamic and descriptive meanings. 'Democracy' refers to certain constitutional arrangements, but it also carries an expression of approval. 'Fascism' refers to a theory of man and a (supposedly connected) corporatist arrangement, but it also expresses disapproval and has been applied to communists and to liberal capitalists. Words are weapons of considerable rhetorical power. Precision and clarity are often superseded by political commitment and ambition as words are stretched well beyond their limits to show that this socialist regime is a democracy or that leader is a fascist. One of the principle moves in this game is what Stevenson called 'persuasive definition', the redefinition of terms to suit one's own moral or political values. When persuasive definition takes place among people who share the same values, semantic absurdity often results: unemployment becomes an act of 'violence' or pornography a form of 'pollution' or an economic theory an 'obscenity'.

The study of politics is bedevilled by the emotive properties of language, but they are not the source of all its problems. A problem of equal magnitude is the interdependence between political propositions and political realities, so that unlike scientists and historians (most of the time) the student of politics may well affect reality with his statements and investigations. People are made more 'politically conscious', however marginally, by being subjected to surveys of opinion. What academics say about the class structure affects what people believe about the class structure and therefore the class structure itself. A statement locating power in a particular group or institution (for instance, the British Civil Service or the International Jewish Conspiracy) cannot fail to have some effect on that group or institution. The historian cannot, by definition, affect his subject;

the scientist does so merely by investigating only in rare cases, like the use of an electron microscope.

Perhaps the central example of interdependence is Robert Merton's idea of the self-fulfilling prophecy where the belief that x is or will be the case has the effect of bringing x about. The most obvious examples come from economics, from markets, whether in money, stocks, commodities or anything else. The belief that prices are rising or going to rise causes people to act in such a way (buying, holding) that prices do rise. If people believe there is going to be high and increasing inflation they will get rid of money, accumulate goods, put up their own charges and wage demands. But there are some political examples almost as clear: the belief that the Mafia or the Vice-Chancellor or the Prime Minister possess great power is likely to lead to them being treated as if they had great power. In politics, though, this does not *necessarily* mean that their power will be enhanced. The opposite may happen – it may be successfully attacked – because self-denying prophecy is also a real possibility in politics; it is a very remote possiblity in market economics.

Self-fulfilling prophecies are often discussed as if they are normally single propositions: 'the price of x is rising'; 'y has enough influence to secure the nomination'; 'z is an unintelligent child'. But just as common, and far more important, are self-fulfilling analyses, entire bodies of theory and expression which can come to be real because they are believed. In economics, there is an important relation between prevailing economic theory and the working of the economy: the Keynesian economy can only work if Keynes is believed. In politics there are many examples: fundamental assumptions about human nature are likely to be self-fulfilling. But the most dramatic examples come from class analyses. Class-consciousness does not exist, in one important sense, unless people believe themselves to be members of separate classes. What people believe about social class is partly a consequence of what sociologists, polemicists and politicians tell them about class. Whether 'all history is the history of class struggles', as Marx and Engels' simplest formulation put it, is true, depends on whether it is believed.

So the social observer cannot confine himself to mere observation except, perhaps, by the highly unnatural expedient of talking only to himself. For this reason and because he is likely to have sincere polemical ambitions, to wish to change the world and think it right that he should try to change the world, he is not restricted to mere truth. This is an important aspect of what Marx meant by the unity of theory and practice. It is also part of the basis of the 'critical theory' developed in Germany by Jürgen Habermas and Theodor Adorno, who see the role of the social theorist as 'interpretative' and 'diagnostic' in a world in which 'false consciousness' is the normal condition.

Sometimes, social theorists argue at cross-purposes when one regards his account of society as detached and the other does not. The committed theorist might say, for instance, 'The Northern Ireland situation is one of intense but disguised class struggle.' The empirical observer would contradict this and point out (rightly in his own terms) 'That's just not true. According to all our evidence and whichever way you define it, Northern Ireland has one of the lowest levels of class affiliation in Europe.' To which a third party, who understands the methods of both, might add, 'Yes, but if he goes on saying it, it might *become* true. . . .'

A further complication to the use of political language is the phenomenon of the obsessive concept. By this I mean words and associated images with which people become obsessed and in terms of which they insistently conceive their experience, irrespective of whether it is fruitful or meaningful to do so. So far as I know, the phrase 'obsessive concept' is my own, but it owes a great deal to the work of J. L. Austin:

> We become obsessed with 'truth' when discussing statements just as we become obsessed with 'freedom' when discussing conduct. So long as we think that what has always and alone to be decided is whether a certain action was done freely or was not, we get nowhere: but as soon as we turn instead to the numerous other adverbs used in the same connection ('accidentally', 'unwillingly', 'inadvertently' etc.) things become easier and we come to see that no concluding inference of the form 'Ergo, it was done freely (or not freely)' is required. Like freedom, truth is a bare minimum or illusory ideal. . . .
> (J. L. Austin, 'Truth')

The nature of conceptual obsession is that we want to know about a thing even when we know that there is nothing to know. Wealth and intelligence are obsessive; so are God and happiness. In politics there are many obsessive concepts: power and democracy are two of the most important in contemporary theory. We want to know who has power over us or how democratic a particular political system is, even though we may realise, at one level, that these are imprecise and unanswerable questions and that we would have more chance of producing coherent answers if we confined ourselves to questions about accountability, the nature of political education and the structure of organised interests.

HOW TO TALK ABOUT POLITICS

Given the tortuous mess which is all we have for a political language, what can be done? The many approaches on offer can be grouped together as four basic strategies.

Reconstruction

Perhaps the most obvious move, given the difficulties of political language, is to construct a new language. After all, other disciplines have successfully progressed by devising new 'conceptual frameworks', most notably economics. Economists have long ago stopped talking about a 'just price' – while political theorists still use concepts of the same antiquity – in favour of developing a technical language to suit their explanatory and diagnostic purposes. Sociologists and psychologists have also developed technical languages. The greatest effort at reconstructing the language of politics has been invested by the large industry of American political science. But advances have been made in several different directions at once, a reflection of the rambling and ill-defined area of the study of politics and the diversity of people who study it. In the 1960s the language of systems theory, laced with many non-ordinary terms such as cybernetics, feedback, input, subsystem, eufunction and dysfunction became an important part of the study of politics. The expansion took place in conjunction with that in the subjects it drew upon for inspiration such as biology, ecology and communications theory. Since then, a major movement has been the revival and expansion of rational models of man which, like those of the economists, have given complete accounts of political action based on the assumption of rational egoism, including some sophisticated developments of theories of strategies and games.

It cannot be said that these tendencies have been a complete failure. They have expanded the ways of looking at politics and in some cases have achieved a local pre-eminence in explanation: for instance strategic theories offer some of the most rewarding accounts of certain kinds of war and committee activity. But judged as candidates for the post of paradigm or dominant style of politics, they have failed. They have not replaced the mess of styles and concepts which is political language, but merely added to it. Perhaps this is for bad reasons: there are too many vested interests and entrenched methods. There are also good reasons. A precise and technical language about politics simply cannot capture the range of things which people want to say about the subject. I remember reading one attempt to make over the whole subject along the lines of rational models, Riker and Ordeshook's *Introduction to Positive Political Theory*, before a seminar began in an American university. A distinguished German professor of politics asked me what I was reading and wagged his finger at the book. 'Conclusive proof that Riker has lost interest in politics', he said.

There is another form of reconstruction, most completely exemplified by Felix Oppenheim's book *Political Concepts*, which is subtitled 'A Reconstruction'. Oppenheim tries to create a neutral and precise language from the words we already use: 'power', 'equality', 'interests', 'welfare' and so on. The two aspects of this exercise are essential to each other: strictly defined meanings which are rigidly separated from any evaluative implications. We can define what 'equality' is and then, as a quite separate exercise, discuss whether it is a good or a bad thing and in what circumstances. Personally, I am sympathetic to this exercise. It fits the canons of logic much better than most political theory. In practice, though, it is like constructing a theory of magnetism and expecting the theory to stop the tide coming in. It would take a great deal more than a professor with a clear mind and a typewriter to change the nature of political language. The emotive nature of political language means that terms will always be persuasively defined and counter-defined, because they have value, real power in a real world. The obsessive quality of concepts means that people will always reject precise and technical meanings by saying, 'But that isn't what liberty (or power or interests) *really* means. . . .' The interdependence of language and action is such that it will always be in many people's interests to stretch the concepts of truth and coherence.

'Reconstruction' could only be achieved in one of two conditions. Either the professor doing the reconstructing must be given a control over education and expression in excess of any experienced so far in history, or theorists should isolate themselves completely from politicians and polemicists. Sufficient control is not possible and would be undesirable if it were. Isolation would render the philosophers useless and the non-philosophers even less well disciplined, semantically, than they are already.

Contestability

In 1956 W. B. Gallie published an essay on 'Essentially Contested Concepts' which was later to become famous and influential, particularly in the study of politics. The central tenet was that 'there are concepts which are essentially contested, concepts the proper use of which inevitably involves endless disputes about their proper uses on the part of their users.' These concepts were to be found particularly in the philosophical problems associated with aesthetics, politics, history and religion. 'Art', 'democracy' and 'a Christian life' are central examples. Gallie outlines the main characteristics of an essentially contested concept. They are appraisive, in that they attribute a quality which is valued. They are internally complex, can be broken down into several variables and discussed in a whole or in parts. They can be modified with changing circumstances and their contested quality (though not necessarily its *essential* status) is recognised. Finally there are two important criteria which are less widely recognised. There must exist an 'original exemplar', something which is accepted by everybody as an undoubtedly genuine example of what the concept means. And there must also be a 'probability and plausibility' that continuous competition allows for the maintenance or development of the 'original exemplar's achievement'.

The idea of essentially contested concepts has considerable appeal. When compared with reconstructionism, it seems much closer to the style and spirit of political argument, its complexity and eternity. The idea has the further merit of establishing the propriety and necessity of argument and disagreement about the

fundamentals of politics. Whereas reconstructionism has an authoritarian ring and implies, at least sometimes, that disagreement can
be damaging to the discourse because it attacks the basic assumptions without which we cannot make progress, contestability looks
liberal: it establishes disagreement as the essence of the discourse.
For these reasons, the idea has exercised considerable appeal and has
been taken up by many writers and used as the basis for an analysis
of political concepts by William Connolly in *The Terms of Political
Discourse*.

The idea does not really work. At its core is a contradiction
between the acceptance that arguments are 'endless' and the stipulation that they should be fruitful. This is very clear when Gallie
compares the contesting of concepts with the competition between
scientific hypotheses. The differences are more important than the
similarities. There are precise rules for the elimination of hypotheses;
disputes are not endless, but are won and lost and come to an end. In
science, progress and resolution can result from argument: Gallie
and his supporters do not demonstrate that these can come from
conceptual contest. The sceptic is entitled to think that there are
many more 'radically confused concepts' (Gallie's phrase) than the
theory allows and that it is not rational to argue about these. He is
also entitled to point out that even the cases Gallie cites do not have
proper 'original exemplars'. Athens is not an uncontroversial
example of democracy, certainly not in a way relevant to the
modern world. Christ cannot be the 'original exemplar' of a
Christian life: he was divine and frequently said so. But who else?
St. Peter? St. Paul? We know little about them and what we know is
controversial. At its worst the theory of contestability is a recommendation that we should discuss what cannot be rationally discussed, that academics should spend their lives dressing their
prejudices, dreams and resentments in the clothes of philosophy.

Transcendentalism

'For the moment, anyway, political philosophy is dead.' Peter
Laslett made this statement in 1956 in what was to become a
famous, even notorious introduction to the first series of his collec-
tions of essays called *Philosophy, Politics and Society*. 'Philosophy' was
taken by Laslett and his readers to be the same thing as 'theory'. He
did not mean that nobody was doing any theorising or philoso-

phising about politics; actually at that time, philosophers and other students of politics were drawing on psychology and anthropology to produce quite original theories of politics. What he meant was that political theory in its 'big' sense was no longer being practised – political theory in its 'grand', 'classical' or 'over-arching' sense. Political theory in the grand sense is the investigation of the fundamental truths about man and society and their implications for the organisation of the state.

Laslett was in no doubt about who killed political philosophy. Although the horrors of the second world war and the advance of sociology formed a hostile environment, 'The Logical Positivists did it. It was Russell and Wittgenstein, Ayer and Ryle. . .'. It is fair to point out that only one of this quartet (Ayer) was a well-defined and self-ascribed logical positivist, though this is something of a detail, because all four were sympathetic to the kinds of criticism which logical positivists made of grand political theory (along with grand moral philosophy, theology, aesthetics and others).

These criticisms were not new. The case of logical positivism (and against political philosophy) was well put by Hume in the eighteenth century at the end of his *Inquiry concerning Human Understanding*:

> If we take in our hand any volume – of divinity or school metaphysics, for instance – let us ask, *Does it contain any abstract reasoning concerning quantity or number?* No. *Does it contain any experimental reasoning, concerning matter of fact and existence?* No. Commit it then to the flames, for it can contain nothing but sophistry and illusion.

Logical positivism admits of three categories of proposition: (1) Formal relations between ideas, such as logic and arithmetic. (2) Well-defined empirical information, such as biology or chemistry. (3) Rubbish, hot air. Clearly, grand political philosophy *et al.* are in category (3).

Yet logical positivism, in any strict sense, is now itself dead. Sir Alfred Ayer has said simply that 'It was wrong.' With the snake dead, the chickens can breed. Political philosophy has had a considerable revival, going from strength to strength since the late 1960s. The two leading American figures of the revival are John Rawls and Robert Nozick. John Rawls's *A Theory of Justice* was

described by the *Times Literary Supplement* as 'the most notable
contribution to (political philosophy) since Sidgwick and Mill'. It
sets out to calculate the proper principles and arrangements of a
society on the basis of what a rational man would accept in advance,
from behind a 'veil of ignorance' (ignorance, that is, about what his
own position in society might be). It is thus a fundamental and a
contractual theory and fits more or less neatly into the grand
tradition. Nozick's *Anarchy, State and Utopia* is fundamentally
similar because it seeks to 'hypothetically explain' the state by
asking the question 'What kind of state could man accept as enhan-
cing his rights?' Man must be said to have rights in the (hypothetical)
condition of being outside the state. Not only is he real in an
important sense in which the state is not, but it is obvious that the
worst state is worse than the worst non-state: the extermination
camp is more fearful than the desert.

   The principles and arrangements which both arrive at are recognisably 'liberal', though in different senses. Nozick's liberalism is a
classical or nineteenth-century sort, called conservative in America.
He favours a minimal state, strong protection of private property
and, therefore, the possibility of a highly inegalitarian distribution
of property, and a purely private provision of medicine. For Nozick,
the state is only preferable to anarchy if it confines itself to the
policing of the *status quo*. His theory has been stigmatised as the
philosophical back-up for the political views of the average Mid-
Western gas station owner. Rawls is more recognisably 'centrist':
his arrangements are similar to those espoused by many Social
Democrats in Europe and 'liberal' Democrats in the United States,
because he insists that the welfare of the least well off person in
society is a crucial criterion in his formulation of arrangements, an
insistence which has led many to interpret his writing as essentially
anti-utilitarian.

ON THE TRANSCENDENTAL

Logical positivism held that:

   1 Language is such that it is possible to produce propositions
      which are linguistically proper but which are not susceptible
      to any kind of test in respect of their truth.

2 In the significant intellectual sense of the word, such propositions lack 'meaning': there is no point, and, in one sense, no content, to investigating or discussing them.

3 Propositions which can be said to have meaning (in the significant sense) fall into two categories:
(a) Empirical
(b) Formal

The successful attacks on logical positivism have said, in effect, that it is incoherent because it does not allow us enough intellectual equipment to make sense of the universe. So the mainstream of philosophy has amended and extended proposition (3) by reviving a further category – the transcendental.

Transcendental knowledge consists of the discovery of the necessary essential and unavoidable structures which determine how mental beings must perceive and discuss the universe. It is what Immanuel Kant called 'synthetic *a priori*' knowledge and Peter Strawson calls the 'preconditions of discourse'. The existence of consciousness and its systematic perception (thus the existence of 'men' and of 'things'), the existence of causation, of space, of dimension and time are the *sorts* of things which can be transcendentally established. And, a good joke on the positivists, the necessity of meaning and the intellectual value of truth are demonstrable only by transcendental argument.

The revivers of 'real' political theory must be talking about the transcendental, because neither side is claiming that political theoretical knowledge is either formal or empirical. They must be saying, when they talk, as some of them do, about natural rights, that 'Human beings must be treated as if they have certain rights and one cannot coherently discuss humans unless these rights are assumed. To ignore these rights is not merely a question of differing from us on values, it is false, a philosophical error.'

But transcendental argument cannot extend to politics. It tells us only that there exist symbolically communicating 'conscious' beings, not whether these beings have further unique properties nor (for example) whether there can be human societies without politics. All other statements about man are empirical observations or moral judgements. The existence of man as a mental entity sets only the bounds of coherence and thus the existence of dimension, causation and ourselves. It has no moral content, nor does it imply even the existence of morality. We cannot conceive of man not having a conception of 'self', but we can conceive of man not having any moral beliefs. The transcendental goes nowhere near far enough for political theory.

The reaction to Rawls's book has contained a strange contradiction. It has been highly praised, far more so than Nozick's or those of other contemporaries. But virtually all the critics who have praised it have seen fundamental flaws in it, saying that the status of the theory is highly unclear. Many have pointed out that his requirements of 'rationality' covertly include important values, most notably an aversion to risk. Others argue that the 'original position' behind a 'veil of ignorance' is inconceivable and nothing substantive can be inferred from it. The principles produced by his arguments have been attacked on the grounds that they not only are open to interpretation, but say nothing substantive without the injection of fundamental value judgements. For example:'inequalities are arbitrary unless it is reasonable to expect that they will work out for everyone's advantage and provided the positions and offices to which they attach, or from which they may be gained, are open to all.' 'Reasonable'? 'Advantage'? 'Open to all'? There is more than a suspicion that the principle is plastic enough to be moulded into any shape. It is all reminiscent of the familiar story of the Emperor's clothes, except that this time the crowd are divided in their opinion. Some are saying, 'What a beautiful shirt. But why are his feet bare?' and others 'Lovely cloak. Pity he has no trousers.' In the background are men rubbing their hands and saying 'It's done wonders for the cloth trade, all this.' But there is nobody who thinks the Emperor is properly dressed.

Conceptual scepticism

It is the minimal position of the conceptual sceptic that at least some of the central terms of political discourse have no meaning in any important and useful sense of that word. At least some of the major questions about politics cannot be answered coherently and some well-established academic debates are a waste of time. By way of explanation, one can point to a major contradiction in the functions of language which is especially acute in the political field, broadly defined. That contradiction lies between man's intellectual search for truth, precision and validity on the one hand and his needs to persuade and to seek grand and over-arching frameworks on the other.

The conceptual sceptic's view of the role of the philosopher is sharply different from that of others. Not for him the discovery of the fundamental and substantive principles of politics, nor jousting in an endless and glorious conceptual tournament nor rebuilding the whole structure of language. He is left doing a bit of this and a bit of that, occasionally discovering a clear rule or convention in the language, frequently criticising and taking to pieces the arguments of others, very often confining himself to the 'negative' role of eradicating error, then overlapping into the sociology of knowledge as he seeks to understand why people argue as they do.

Much of the rest of this book is primarily a development and application of conceptual scepticism. It may be a 'negative' activity in many ways, but it is also demanding and satisfying.

4

SCIENCE AND
RELIGION

SCIENCE

Science is the systematic attempt to explain the universe. It follows that there is a doctrine of uniformity which is essential to the nature of science. This doctrine used to be called 'the uniformity of nature': Harrington's expression in the seventeenth century was that 'What neither is, nor never was, in nature, never can be in nature.' But now it is expressed as 'the uniformity of science': Stephen Toulmin says that 'It is not nature which is uniform, but science, and uniform only in that it is methodical and self-correcting. . . .'

The central point in either interpretation is that science seeks a universality of explanation. This is quite different from the criteria we often use in explaining things in practice. Suppose, to take the Newtonian example, we ask the question 'Why did that apple fall from its tree?' We might reply:

'It's autumn.'
'It was too heavy.'
'It was over-ripe.'
'The wind blew it off.'

For most psychological and practical purposes these explanations would do: they might remove most people's curiosity about the matter and suggest some recommendations about how to look after apples or when to pick them. But, from a scientific point of view, these explanations are fundamentally flawed in two ways. First, there is the question of the meaning of terms like 'autumn', 'wind' and 'heavy' and the danger of a circularity in which 'autumn' is a time at which apples fall off, wind a phenomenon defined as removing apples (windfalls) from trees and 'heaviness' a condition in which they tend to fall off. Then there is the inability of any of these kinds of explanation to provide satisfactory answers to questions like 'Do apples always fall off trees in autumn?' and their successors: 'Well, why did this one?'

None of the explanations is a universal: some apples stay on their trees all winter, till they rot, despite high winds and frost. Even if we were to stipulate a very precise range of conditions (time, variety of apple, direction of wind and so on) we only raise the probability of the apple falling. There remains a possibility, however remote, that something outside our specified conditions – a bolt of lightning, human agency or whatever – will intervene to prevent the apple falling. Anyway, what does 'falling' mean?

What satisfies the scientific aspiration, as opposed to idle curiosity or the practical need to have a rule of thumb, is something of the following kind:

'Why did A happen?'
'Because B happened.'
'How do you know there is a connection between A and B?'
'Events of type a always follow events of type b.'

Thus it is in the nature of science that it cannot confine itself to the 'ordinary' or 'natural' language, but must construct new ways of looking at the universe, so for instance, 'mass' and 'gravity' replace 'apples' and 'trees' in the search for universal regularity. This is not just the replacement of words by words but of one framework, system, and idea of reality by another.

The entire procedure of science is based on the assumption that the universe is fundamentally regular, provided we can see it in the right way. But why? Unless we resort to referring to the divine will, the assumption that there are laws which govern the universe seems optimistic and unnecessary. That was what was wrong with the 'uniformity of nature': it saw the necessity of regularity as being part of the universe, like stars or planets. But the assumption is really part of science: the activity cannot exist, we cannot conduct a rational search for coherence, unless we make it. Uniformity is an absolutely necessary assumption of the investigation of the universe, not a fact about the thing investigated.

The assumption of regularity does not imply that any particular conceptual framework satisfies the aspiration of regularity. Scientific evidence normally can be incorporated into the accepted framework; sometimes the framework must be reformed or reinterpreted, but on very rare occasions it must be replaced, built-under as the basis of science. These occasions are what Thomas Kuhn called 'scientific revolutions' and the most recent was when the discoveries of Einstein and others led to the replacement of the Newtonian structure of mass and gravity by a framework which consists, fundamentally, of energy and space. Science is never finished and there is no reason to suppose it ever will be. At any one time it must answer some questions of the form 'Why is that pattern of energy-in-space always followed by this one?' by answers which say, in effect, 'That's just the way it is, one of the fundamental relations of the universe.' But whereas the form is necessary, the particular answer is not.

Man is flesh and blood, carbon and hydrogen, and thus, energy in space. There is no question of his not being physical, nor of his being left out of the assumption of uniformity. Scientifically he exists, he is part of the universe, unlike gods and ghosts. And yet the systematic and universal character of scientific explanation does not guarantee a satisfactory explanation when it comes to dealing with men. For instance, if one is curious as to why Hitler hated the Jews, there is no satisfaction whatever in saying that it was a question of his chromosomes or the consequences of a brain tumour. Partly, this is a practical limitation: Hitler is dead, he was very powerful when he was alive; arguably, it would be morally wrong, even if he were powerless, to conduct the kind of physical investigation of his being which would explain his behaviour. All three possibilities suggest difficulties about a scientific explanation of his behaviour.

But the unsatisfactoriness of science is not merely a consequence of its practical limitations. Even if, by some inconceivable step, we could go back in time and fully investigate Hitler and discover some source of his behaviour which was physical, we would still be entitled to say: But I still don't understand. Why the Jews? What sort of person was he? The paradox is that science explains man with unique propriety, as it explains everything else, yet it does not explain man at all.

The paradox can only be resolved by the recognition that we have two logically separate discourses. The scientific discourse has a necessary assumption that it aspires to be (and therefore in a sense *is*) a complete and systematic account of the universe. It is therefore hierarchical: science does not normally talk in terms of the fundamental constituents of the universe, but it does talk in terms (for instance, chemical, biological and engineering terms) which can be reduced to such fundamentals. Science talks about men as part of the universe.

In contrast, the social discourse talks about men as men, positing that they have minds (rather than brains) and that they make choices and perform actions (as opposed to exhibiting patterns of behaviour). The social discourse has no fundamental nor necessary structure; it is incomplete even as an account of its own limited subject-matter and it is egalitarian. Random events occur in society: important men go mad or are struck by lightning, vital messages fail to arrive because of storms or earthquakes. There are no social explanations for these social events; they are reminders that society exists in a physical context. By contrast, every physical event must be assumed to have a physical explanation. The branches and forms of the social discourse relate to each other as a jumbled confusion of rivalry, complement and overlap. Sociology does not reduce to psychology, nor politics to economics. To some extent these disciplines must regard the others as mistaken in their emphasis or assumptions: there must be *some* conflict, for example, between an understanding of man which starts with his membership of collective entities (like families and classes) and one which starts with the structure of a single mind.

Distinguishing between a social and a scientific discourse does not imply that there are two universes, one containing 'minds' and the other 'bodies', nor that man is a 'ghost in a machine'. There are two logically distinct ways of talking about the same entities: in that sense, and that sense alone, 'dualism' is inevitable. There are, necessarily, rivalries and conflicts between social and scientific discourse. In a sense, the history of ideas has been the forward march of science from a time when the minds of gods and demons were assumed to explain thunderstorms and volcanoes to one in which much human behaviour can be explained physically. Contemporary psychology sees the world in terms of both discourses: psychoanalysis is an exploration of the soul while neurophysiology is an adjunct of physics.

The human way to understand humans is to put oneself 'in their shoes', to look at the world through their eyes. The understanding of Hitler's hatred of the Jews consists in a clear view of what Hitler saw when he looked at the world. This stretching out into the minds of others is the special meaning which Max Weber gave to the German world *verstehen* or understanding. It is what some philosophers call 'introspective analogy'.

It is by no means so well regulated as scientific discovery. We can never know for certain whether we have done it right and there will always be conflicting, or simply different, insights into the actions of any man or group of men. All we can do, in Weber's terms, is to construct a 'plausible story' and to 'check it against the facts'. It is no good imagining that the poor of Paris revolted in 1789 because they were getting poorer and, therefore, more desperate, when there is factual evidence that they were getting richer. We can reject many insights on the grounds of their incompatibility with the facts, but it is rare to be able to reduce alternative accounts to one by this method. It follows from the distinctions already made between the two that the social discourse is 'subjective' in a way that science is not. The quality of the explanation depends partly on the audience to which it is addressed. This is why history must be rewritten every generation: 1640 excites our curiosity in a slightly different way now from the way in which it did in 1950. But sociology and politics must be rewritten every generation as well.

SCIENCE AND POLITICS

There are trivial senses of 'science' in terms of which a social science is possible. But in the important sense of 'science', the systematic investigation of the universe, there can be no genuinely 'social' science, no science which deals with human beings in human terms. The most crucial consequences of this for politics are negative: our political and moral options cannot be closed by any notion of 'inexorable' laws, or 'objective' reality or 'inevitable' conditions. History has no undercurrent of 'progress' which cannot be denied; there is no final state which man will inevitably reach. In society we make our own reality; only in the physical universe do we have to accept what we are given. Nothing is written, except physics, and we cannot read all of the writing.

This has consequences for our sense of responsibility, both individual and collective. Science, causation and inevitability are logically separate from choice. Men must be assumed to have choices if we are to understand them as men. Illness or social deprivation may excite our compassion, but they do not preclude the existence of choice and the responsibility of the individual for his actions. Only when something is not an action at all, where there is no consciousness, can the individual be said to have no responsibility for what he does. But then, in cases where a man is, for instance, completely drugged, he cannot be said to 'do' anything at all. By extension, we can be said to be collectively responsible for the fate of our own society, though it is difficult to attribute that responsibility and therefore to give it moral meaning. The important thing about collective respnsibility is not that any one person, or even anybody at all, can choose what sort of society he wants to be part of. It is that it can never be right to accept any social tendency or circumstance as being inexorable in the sense of being altogether beyond the bounds of human choice.

Science is man's 'highest' aspiration in the sense of being his most distinctively human activity, because it takes language and logic as far as they can be taken. It is above politics and logically independent of social considerations. This does not mean that scientists ought to conduct any experiments on human beings which will enhance scientific understanding: their *conduct* is not above moral judgement. What it does men is that science should always be rigorously independent of ideology. Astronomy cannot be 'heretical' (which is what the Catholic church said of Galileo); physics cannot be 'bourgeois' (which is what the Communist Party of the Soviet Union called Einstein). The discovery of new biological differences between races can only be precluded on biological grounds, not on moral or political ones. A respect for science is the best protection against the worst of ideology.

RELIGION

Alan Ryan, writing in *New Society*, has eloquently expressed a mystery which has baffled many irreligious scholars:

Who has never been puzzled by teachers and colleagues who spend five days a week in the laboratory, professionally committed to the enterprise of unravelling the mysteries of nature in the most purely secular way, and who then spend Sunday on their knees praising a deity who is explicitly said to operate in mysterious ways and to work by miraculous intervention? Are they mad? Are they schizophrenic? It would be stretching words to say so: their characters may generally seem to be models of integration. And yet they live in two different universes and operate with two incompatible belief systems. If one person can do so, how much more a whole society.

Religious belief is notoriously difficult to define. Many apparent definitions turn out, on examination, to be banal insights into the religious state of mind rather than distinctions between religious belief and non-religious belief. For instance, Schliermacher: 'The essence of religion consists in the feeling of absolute dependence.' Or Whitehead: 'Religion is what the individual does with his own solitariness.'

It is not possible to provide a covering definition of all the states of belief which might be called religion and whose claims could not be logically eliminated. It seems more reasonable to regard 'religion' as being like 'sport' in covering a wide variety of overlapping uses not susceptible to a single definition. Quite apart from its historical complexity, the meaning of the word becomes 'stretched' in contemporary debate, like many others which have moral and political implications. But it is easy to indicate the main properties of religion in the sense which it is important to consider religion in trying to understand politics. It is a belief in the supernatural, of a kind of truth which is not science, but which is above and beyond science. Most typically, it is theism, the belief in a God or single conscious mind which is responsible for the universe, and a proper object of worship and from whose will moral precepts are drawn.

Religion, in this sense, is potentially a more complete account of the universe than is science, because it can say things about men as men, which science cannot. But it is rarely treated as such. The devoutly religious still keep their powder dry; as Alan Ryan says, religious devotion 'seems entirely consistent with being able to master a gunnery manual'. Religious belief has been the 'normal' state of man. It falls very clearly, though, into two quite different spirits. I will refer to these as *serious* religion and *formal* religion. By serious religion I mean belief which is literal, which stresses that the supernatural exists in the same way, or in a clearer or 'higher' way, than the natural: God is more real than a tree. Morally, serious religion insists that God's commands and requirements (including, usually, belief in himself) supersede all other judgements. In Christianity, it means asking 'What does Jesus say?', then getting an answer, at least sometimes, whether from the Church, the Bible or from personal revelation and being prepared to act on that answer. It means that the answer must be taken as binding whatever its conflict with social convention, personal judgement and concepts of reasonableness.

Serious religion is the curse of humanity. It is worthy of the most complete contempt from the conservative thinker; it conflicts with his suspicion of the Absolute, his *prima facie* attitude to scepticism, his belief that the essence of a man's existence is his place and culture, his insistence on the primacy and independence of moral judgement. It is fair to say that serious religion appeals to many of the least admirable traits in man: his desire for easy answers to moral and philosophical questions, his inability to accept dispute, his search for a basis on which to impose rigid rules of conduct. And, of course, serious religion is simply *wrong*. God does not exist in the same ways as energy or truth; if he exists at all, it is in a much weaker sense. Religious accounts of the universe do not satisfy the same canons of coherence and consistency as do those of science. There is considerable force in the logical positivist's assertion that religious propositions do not mean anything: there are no proper criteria for the application of religious terms. 'God' is not a concept in the way that 'energy' or even 'the working class' are. It is just a word, which covers a range of images and has formal relations with other words like 'creator' and 'omniscient'. On the other hand, the logical positivists clearly over-stated the case, at least formally: this range of connotations and formal relations is a 'meaning' of sorts. There is more than one meaning to 'meaning'. But an important point still holds: 'God' and 'Hell' and 'salvation' and 'transubstantiation' do not mean anything in the logical and scientific scheme of meaning. Or if they do, religion is false: the biscuit does *not* turn to flesh; there is no 'life' after death.

However liberal the holders of serious religious belief may claim to be personally, their religion is itself a threat to human liberty and diversity. By definition Hell is either the greatest deprivation conceivable or a deprivation greater than anything conceivable. If we take it seriously, anything would be justified in the cause of salvation. Truth, in its most important sense, becomes something which is not concerned with reason and dispute and evidence, but with a moral and spiritual commitment. It is not something to seek and discover, but something to accept. Paradoxically, serious religion reduces many important arguments to a comic triviality. Moral guilt becomes a matter of the spots on a goat's liver, truth a question of the precise meaning of a word in a dead language.

On the face of it Christianity would seem to be a religion difficult, if not impossible, to take seriously. It is peculiarly ambiguous and therefore difficult to be serious about (at least, collectively). It has been claimed to be a religion of firmness and flexibility, of peace and of war, of community and of solitude, of authority and of anarchy. One is entitled to ask, 'Is there nothing which Christianity as such can not be said to stand for?' The answer is 'No. Absolutely nothing'. It has been interpreted as justifying the most horrific tortures and the most bloodthirsty wars, chastity and licentious liberation. The moral consequences of its various interpretations are quite limitless; it would be arbitrary to rule anything out of court.

There are many sources of ambiguity in Christianity. Christ himself sounds at times like a quietist and a Tory ('Render unto Caesar . . .'), yet he attacks those who are making a living in the fiscal sector with physical violence. He emerges from the different gospels as a subtly different personality. There is always a doubt about the status of the Old Testament, largely the legends and laws of a nationalistic and violent pastoral tribe, in flat contradiction to much of what is in the New Testament, yet somehow valid nevertheless. Since the Bible was completed, the religion has absorbed a wealth of Greek philosophy and Roman practice and the lore and custom of a thousand tribes. A religion difficult to take seriously, one would think, but many have succeeded in this difficult task.

Such condemnation of religion in general and Christianity in particular in the name of conservatism will undoubtedly seem odd to many. Is not religion the opiate of the people and the Anglican Church the Tory party at prayer? In most of continental Europe the intellectual and political links between conservatism and catholicism have been inextricable and highly durable. But I am talking about conservatism in the English tradition and about *serious* religion.

Much religion is merely *formal*. There are various aspects of the hiving-off of religious practices and propositions to a formal status. Philosophically, the essence of religious formality is the complete logical separation of religious propositions from other propositions including those of science and morality. God 'exists', but this is not the same kind of existence that other beings have. Although he has things to say, they do not impinge on the pursuit of science or the operation of a personal conscience. The theory of evolution and its consequences (including the implication that the Bible is basically wrong about the age of the earth) represents no detraction from God's status. His Creation is to be understood as something quite distinct from scientific accounts of the origins of the earth and universe. He may have recommended turning the other cheek, but clearly didn't mean this to apply to foreign invaders or bullies who need a good hiding.

Formal religion inverts the primacy of theology which serious religion requires. It asks 'What is true?', 'What is right?', 'What do *we* stand for?' and then erects God as a conceptual statue to our finer feelings and higher aspirations. The difficulty of taking Christianity seriously is an advantage when what is required is a highly plastic framework for the expression of our feelings. There are many advantages to formal religion. It does offer people the great collective expression of their class, tribal and national solidarities. In the village church and the school chapel when the hymns are sung, the whole can be greater than the parts, the spirit can be more than its mere context. The flexibility of Christianity amounts to a kind of spiritual promiscuity. In the non-conformist chapels of the nineteenth century it served as a recharging of the spiritual values of the self-made man, who considered charity uncharitable. In the churches of Ireland and Poland, Christian ceremonies become expressions of national loyalty and independence. Among the men of certain British regiments Christian hymns are sung as an expression of a loyal and violent masculine collective. In Westminster Abbey on state occasions they can be celebrations of a national identity to which institutional continuity is central.

But the feelings which religion inspires go beyond anything which can be expressed as mere group mores. We all have feelings which stress the significance of our lives which cannot be expressed. Feelings of love, of intense joy, of the beauty of landscape or of music, feelings of nostalgia; strange feelings, which combine all of these and more and which cannot really be expressed at all. Religion, in a great common cause with art, is an expression of these feelings. Where it has allowed itself to become the expression of such non-doctrinal urges, religion has been the catalyst of wonderful things, of fine music and painting and the great collective aspiration of the cathedrals. It is technically incorrect, but nevertheless useful, to call the feelings which occur on this common ground between religion and art, mysticism. The orthodox definition of mysticism is of personal knowledge of God. I am talking about a feeling which lacks the doctrinal implications of 'knowledge' and the ontological ones of 'God', but which nevertheless is profound, beyond mere verbal expression. Mysticism in this limited sense is not only acceptable, it is an essential of a full and fully rooted life. But its best expression is not theological doctrine, rather a lump in the throat.

Formal religion allows serious argument. It assumes that God is essentially reasonable and that, whatever his pronouncements appear to say, they can be properly interpreted as equivalent to something sensible. Thus it is possible for the General Synod of the Church of England to have a perfectly serious debate about uni-lateral nuclear disarmament, as it did in 1983, in which those who believe in God consider the matter in exactly the same way as if they did not believe in God. It is possible to imagine religious debates about nuclear weapons in which the criteria employed related to the infallibility of one or more persons present, the exact meaning of a Greek or Hebrew phrase or the search for an ominous sign. The Church of England is not, on the whole, like that; it assumes that God could only be a reasonable chap who will fit in with the decisions of other reasonable chaps.

I would still call myself an atheist and not resort to the relatively new (nineteenth-century) self-categorisation of 'agnostic'. Atheism is correct principally because the sense in which God, and other religious entities, exist is neither clear nor useful. There is no such position as being morally religious in accepting God's commands; his word is unclear, prescriptively inadequate. But religion does express some of man's deepest and finest feelings – of collective being and solidarity and of the profound individual relationship between a conscious being and the whole of the universe. But religion is only acceptable so long as it is not serious, so long as it regards its theological doctrine as either something of no import-ance or as logically completely separate from knowledge and morality. The worst of all worlds is one in which religion is serious and godless, in which the body of the Lord is itself transubstantiated into an abstract ideal of the spirit of man, and taken to support pacifism, internationalism and socialism.

5

RIGHT AND WRONG

Having a moral sense means being able to moralise, to express moral opinions, to evaluate actions and systems of action and to prescribe behaviour. So the overwhelming majority of people have a moral sense: they moralise. But a coherent moral sense is rare because it requires two conditions which most people find difficult to meet. The first condition is that moralising should be logically consistent and the second is that it should be genuinely substantive. To moralise in a genuinely substantive way means prescribing something which can be treated as a moral rule and which could be used as the general rule of a society. This requirement is not the same as the criterion of 'universalisability' which Kant and many other moral philosophers have stipulated as necessary to proper or rational moralising. That a moral recommendation should be 'universalisable' requires that it should be capable of being applied to all beings to whom moral propositions apply. The requirement that I am putting forward is weaker: it says only that a recommendation could be the rule for a particular society.

A fully developed moral sense should recognise what morality is. That is, it should recognise that prescribing is prescribing; it is not stating a fact or making an inference from factual premises. To moralise properly is to make a judgement and express it in such a way that it could be used as a rule. There is an ultimate logical separation between truth and morality. (This is not quite the same as insisting on a gap between 'facts' and values because, of course, there are many kinds of truth which are not facts.) David Hume regarded this relation of logical separateness as both important and ignored. He stated it several times:

Reason is the discovery of truth or falsehood. Truth or falsehood consists in an agreement or disagreement either to the *real*
relation of ideas, or to *real* existence and matter of fact. Whatever, therefore, is not susceptible of this agreement or disagreement, is incapable of being true or false, and can never be an
object of our reason. Now 'tis evident our passions, volitions,
and actions, are not susceptible of any such agreement or
disagreement; being original facts and realities, complete in
themselves, and implying no reference to other passions, volitions and actions. 'Tis impossible, therefore, they can be pro-
nounced either true or false, and be either contrary or con-
formable to reason. (David Hume, *A Treatise of Human Nature*,
book III, part 1, section I)

The difference between morality and truth can be expressed in any
of the major terms of philosophy. Moral propositions cannot be
'true' in the sense that it is true that two plus two equals four or that
friesian cows are black and white. We cannot demonstrate that
people who disagree with a moral proposition have failed to understand established conventions or are colour-blind, as we can with
well-formulated truths. Moral entities do not exist in the way that
persons and material objects do. We cannot conduct a discourse
without accepting that these things are *real*. But we could carry on
our lives, at a practical and intellectual level, without accepting that
there were such things as 'rights' or 'wickedness'. Nor can people
'know' morality in the sense that they know information. With
moral propositions we can judge them to be right or merely accept
them or prescribe their consequences or act on them; but we cannot
know them.
    Philosophers are fond of building apparent bridges across the
'gap' between information and morality. Two of the most familiar
are 'Murder is wrong' and 'People ought to keep their promises.'
Virtually all societies prohibit murder and it is difficult to imagine a
society which does not legislate against murder. So the wrongness
of murder seems to be a good candidate for the status of the moral
absolute, the ethical truth. But condemning murder is a formal and
empty act as 'murder' has no descriptive meaning. In the vast
majority of ways in which it is used, it does not mean 'killing'. Most
societies allow men to kill men in self-defence and, by extension, in
war. Many allow killing with an element of concord on the part of

those killed: voluntary euthanasia and far more commonly, over history as a whole, duelling. Abortion, execution and involuntary euthanasia are highly controversial in most contemporary societies. In the past there have been societies which permitted each of these practices and those which condemned them. 'Murder', in its legal sense, is the name we give to the kinds of killing that the law condemns. In its moral sense, it is the name we give to that killing of which we disapprove. To say that British soldiers were involved in murdering Argentinians in the South Atlantic would be rhetorical and provocative, because it contradicts the values which most people hold. To say that abortion is murder is controversial because there is bitter division on the subject. On both of these issues, unless you believe that you have direct and unique word from God, there are no moral truths, only alternative and contentious judgements. It is not always and obviously wrong to kill agents of the civil power; indeed, we applaud it in the context of Afghanistan or occupied France. Many people (and some legal systems) condone the 'crime of passion', typically the killing of one's wife's lover when caught in the act. In 1982 an English judge condoned (in effect) a man killing his wife after she had nagged him vitriolically for 25 years. I have mixed feelings about that; indeed, I would claim that it was symptomatic of having a developed moral sense to have mixed feelings about a wide variety of issues.

So 'Murder is wrong' says nothing substantive. It is a mere semantic equation between two moral terms, reducible to 'wrongful killing is wrong'. The argument about 'People ought to keep their promises' seems more complex. Consider the following inference:

I have promised to do x
Therefore, I have an obligation to do x
Therefore, I ought to do x

But anyone who believed that people ought always to obey their promises might reasonably be described as a moral idiot. We can ignore promises made under duress because, arguably, they are not promises. By way of example, let us say I voluntarily and sincerely promise that I will meet my wife outside a shop at 6 pm and on the way I come across somebody who has collapsed and needs taking to hospital. A promise is definitely an obligation: it is the clearest and most central example of an obligation. Thus, I have an obligation to my wife and none (at least, not in any formal sense) to the person who has collapsed: I owe him nothing. Few people would say that I should meet my obligation to my wife; I do not think I would be alone in saying that to meet my obligation simply because it was an obligation would be fanaticism, whereas to meet it because it was the easier of the two alternatives would be callous. So the third line in the inference does not follow from the second. People ought not always to do what they have an obligation to do. Since all obligations, in the strict sense, are forms of promise, it is extremely important to grasp this relationship. These include debts and contracts (including marriages). Anyone who seriously believed that promises should never be broken should be implacably opposed to divorce. The question 'Under what circumstances should I fulfil my obligations?' is complicated in two dimensions. Not only can it be approached from the point of view of different values, but the circumstances in which the problem arises can vary infinitely. Every person is unique; every moral dilemma occurs only once: substantive answers to moral questions like 'Under what circumstances should I fulfil my obligations?' can come only from judgements and not from principles which are either absolute or absolutely general, nor from computer programs.

I have not discussed obligations to the state. Native-born citizens and subjects (not including commissioned officers and naturalised American citizens) do not have obligations to the state. The question 'When should I obey the state?' is thus more like 'When should I obey my mother?' than it is like 'When should I obey my wife?' Of course, people should obey the state most of the time, but that is not a matter of obligation.

If one accepts the existence of a logical gap between truth and morality, then some kind of relativism follows. By relativism I mean the acceptance that, just as different individuals can have different moral values, so can different societies have different sets or ranges of values which they employ in law and social practice and which they use to legitimise themselves. Furthermore, a relativist must accept that there is no absolute test to which rival sets of values can be put and shown to be right or wrong, nor even better or worse than each other.

But there is relativism and relativism. At one extreme, we can say 'The perpetrator of the action comes from a different society (or culture or nation) to me, so I cannot comment on the action. Nailing men's heads to the floor is an accepted practice among those people. . . .' In contrast, it would be quite consistent to be a relativist who was as intolerant as any absolutist. He might say 'We have got our values and they have got theirs', but he might then add 'and from our point of view it is intolerable that anybody should practise their values, so we are arming ourselves to destroy them.' To the question 'When should one fight against another group or society because they are practising a different set of values?' I suspect that most people would answer, 'Never' and think it was a sensible answer. But it cannot be a serious answer. If we have values at all, there must come a point at which we feel constrained to act because we find the nature of other people's values are so appalling. The Third Reich offers the most generally acceptable example: German Nazism was, undoubtedly, a set of values. But there are many others. Considering the vicious cruelty, corruption and callous incompetence to which Uganda was subjected in the 1970s, we might well conclude that the British Army (or anybody else with enough muscle) should have invaded it and attempted to establish a relatively decent order. That they did not is sound practical politics (and economics), but that does not contradict the moral case for taking action. The same relationship exists between different sub-cultures within one society. A principle of toleration and a value of diversity may be good reasons in themselves for the majority tolerating some practices of which they disapprove. Here, too, there must be limits: the repression of women or children or extreme cruelty to animals or whatever, the elimination of which is judged to be more important than toleration and diversity.

ON LACKING A MORAL SENSE

It is not easy to have a coherent and substantive moral sense. There are so many mistakes which can be made. Perhaps the most familiar is inconsistency – acting and judging on logically incompatible grounds. In moral criticism inconsistency is often very close to dishonesty: in saying that someone is operating a 'double standard' we can mean that he has not thought out logically the relations between the values he is applying in one case and those in another or that he is only holding values so long as they suit his interests or that he is in a state of unclarity or hypocrisy which lies between these two.

But, although the 'double standards' argument is one of the most frequent ploys in moral argument, it is often used unfairly. It is not inconsistent to say that it is wrong for wives to commit adultery, but not for husbands, nor to say (as is more common) that it is trivially wrong for husbands to commit adultery, but seriously wrong for wives. It only becomes inconsistent if you also claim to value the greatest possible identity of treatment of men and women, which has been a minority view over history as a whole and is unlikely to be held by those who overtly favour male adultery but oppose female adultery. In talking of adultery, I have been considering cases in which only the man can be said to be committing adultery: a married man with a single woman. Sexual intercourse between a married man and a married woman has a different status: for the 'chauvinist' to oppose this he would need only to accept the more commonplace value that both partners had complicity in an act of sex that was morally wrong if they both acted voluntarily.

Similarly, it is not inconsistent, nor a 'double standard', for a man to be a millionaire and remain a socialist. It would be fatuous if he were to argue that he was trying to raise everybody to his standard of living: given the nature of money and the relationship between goods and status this would be impossible in any meaningful sense. But he could argue that the cause of socialism would not be enhanced in any way if he were to take a vow of poverty and even that, given the facts about the current corruption and inefficiency of the world, his money would be better looked after by himself. Similarly, a puritan could write pornography without inconsistency: he could argue that pornography would be written whether he wrote it or not and that he would write it in a more humane and literary style.

If 'double standards' are too often cited as a ploy in a moral argument, false standards are not spotted often enough. The commonest form of false standards lies in the equation of moral judgement with something else, its reduction to some kind of information. This happens very often in the religious context where the moral sense is subjugated to authoritative pronouncements and the interpretation of texts. The Christian religions have been as vicious as any in these respects, the Roman Catholic Church by systematically attempting to eradicate the moral feelings of its flock in favour of obedience to the church, and some of the Protestant churches by replacing moral sense with biblical text. It is an easy move from these forms of absolutism to cruelties which people rarely perpetrate when they have only their own judgement to fall back on – the fire, the Inquisition and the wheel.

But secular absolutism can work in exactly the same way. Hitching one's moral wagon to some supposedly objective phenomenon like 'progress', the 'Aryan race' or the 'working class' can amount to the same thing. Perhaps the most total abdication of moral sense is to be found among those who believe in the necessity for complete loyalty to an organisation or 'movement', 'solidarity' or 'unity' as it is often called. The human capacity for slavish adherence to organisations seems almost limitless. All over the world there have been people who reduced all their principles to a total acceptance of the policy of the Communist Party of the Soviet Union. In the case of those who survived a quarter of a century from (say) 1932, they had trailed along (morally speaking) behind the massacre of the Kulaks, the purges and eradication of the Old Bolsheviks, the Nazi-Soviet Pact, the creation of the 'Iron Curtain', the invasion of Hungary. . . .

In some cases such loyalty was comic rather than vicious. I have in mind an old communist couple I knew in my childhood. They were very kind people and very pleasant company. Their devotion to Joseph Stalin was of the most minimal use to him; I am convinced that, given his power, they would never have acted as he did. Their class-based judgements of the world bore no apparent relation to the kindness and courtesy with which they treated people of any class. Theirs is another way in which people can fail to have a coherent morality – holding to a set of values which are quite detached from one's actions, stating the 'necessity' of eradicating the Kulaks while avoiding giving pain to a rabbit. It may be harmless when compared with fanaticism but it is no more coherent.

Some people reduce morality to mere snobbery. The mark of this reduction is often the substitution of words like 'civilised' and 'distasteful' for moral words, so that hanging criminals is dismissed as 'distasteful' and anything which is approved is equated with civilisation, whether it is the principle that wrongdoers should be rehabilitated or an endless willingness to 'negotiate' with one's enemies. 'Civilised' is an odd adjective to choose: in origin it means 'urbanised'; in practice it means 'fashionable'. If there is an overt expression of the assumptions which underly these usages, it is the equation of morality with the current fashions of educated opinion. 'Civilised' carries a connotation of education as well as reasonableness. But educated viciousness is not so rare, being spectacularly evident in the plethora of doctorates with which leading members of the Nazi Party were qualified.

Moral judgement is also suspended if one either raises standards to an unrealistic level or becomes obsessed with a single standard. Both of these mistakes are made simultaneously in many contemporary arguments about 'racism'. In some people's minds 'racism' has become the single great sin which dwarfs all others. It includes many different kinds of action and attitude: it includes the man who dislikes people of a different race and the one who has a set of values and beliefs such that people of a different race are 'inferior' in some respect, alongside the man who attacks the houses and persons of people of different races as well as those who run extermination camps. This is a dangerous trivialisation of morality; people should be judged by what they do, not by what they feel and believe. There are many worse sins than 'racism', in its passive aspect: to equate a failure to cope with immigration with participation in racial extermination is both to blow a normal human reaction out of proportion, and thus to set an unattainable standard, and to trivialise something appalling. A similar, and possibly more repugnant position is held by all those who treat 'violence' as the ultimate sin. The football hooligan, the riot policeman and the political terrorist are all awarded the same shudder of distaste. At least sometimes one of these is engaged in voluntary and limited combat, one is responding to the initiation of violence in the interests of civil order, while the third is wilfully killing and maiming people to express his values, emotions or identity. Of anyone who equates the three, I feel entitled to say that he has no serious capacity for moral judgement.

Prescribing makes no sense unless we can assume that men can respond to moral rules and to threats of punishment: in other words, that they can be held responsible for their actions. Much modern argument undermines the concept of individual responsibility. This is not true of physical science: in principle the completeness of the physical explanation of human behaviour does not preclude the conditions of responsibility; it is logically independent. But it does include much social pseudo-science which explains action in terms of social circumstances and thus transfers responsibility on to 'society'. (An equivalent move, more favoured by conservatives, is to blame 'the parents.') If people cannot be held responsible for their actions, then morality is logically superfluous.

The main point of this chapter has been to stress how difficult it is to have a coherent and developed moral sense, to be able to make judgements which are substantive, in the knowledge that other people will make different judgements. To reach this state one must be capable of treating people as moral agents, of regarding them as responsible. One must studiously avoid equating morality with non-moral entities like God, history, the working class or progress. One must have genuine values and not merely use values as sticks in argument. These values must be relevant and prescribe performable actions. One must be consistent.

It is perfectly possible to have such a sense while being a socialist, whether revolutionary or gradualist; but it is, perhaps, more difficult. It is far easier if one is a person of independent judgement, though firmly rooted in a particular culture and with realistic horizons: in other words, a conservative (though not necessarily a Conservative). Because they have disbarred themselves from having a mature moral sense, some people on the 'left' find it very difficult to argue, to cope with those who fundamentally disagree with them without becoming angry or prematurely contemptuous. The 'right-wing' intellectual, in contemporary Europe at least, is protected from such narrowness and absolutism by having to work in an intellectually hostile enviroment. He is likely to be surrounded by people, varying in quality from the clever and honest to the dim and dishonest, who disagree with him.

6

EQUALITY AND
JUSTICE

In most of the senses one can imagine the statement that 'all men are equal' is clearly false whether 'men' is taken to mean men or persons. They are not equal in strength, cleverness, creativity, character or interest. Nor do they have equal needs or requirements. The statement is no less false if it is changed to 'All men are born equal' or 'All men are created equal.' Even if one interprets 'born' or 'created' in a highly abstract way so that the state of being born or created is quite distinct from the social and economic circumstances of being born or created, people are unequal. Even if we cannot tell the exact borders of 'nature' and 'nurture', we know enough to say that nature, or genetics, is enormously important in determining people's capacities, including their height and intellect and their chances of avoiding cancer or insanity.

So it is not *true* that all men are equal unless we can discover some existing quality of such overwhelming moral importance in respect of which people are equal, that the ways in which they are unequal can be seen, by comparison, as trivial. Philosophy offers several suggestions for this quality. Hobbes suggested that it consisted in the capacity of any one human being to kill any other and consequently in the mutual need for authority. Although different in emphasis this is clearly related to the idea that people are all equal in their social propensity, their need to cooperate. Alternatively, Bentham wrote that 'Each is to count for one and no one is to count for more than one.' Utilitarianism, the morality based on the maximisation of pleasure and the minimisation of pain, was to start from the basis of an equal capacity for pleasure and pain. Everything that we can measure about pleasure and pain is distributed unequally: the ability to withstand pain, the variety of sources of pleasure, the level of sophistication at which either pain or pleasure can be described, and so on. But these can be distinguished from the actual *sensation* of pain or pleasure and there is nothing to refute the argument that if they can be experienced at all they can be experienced equally. Finally, many egalitarians would suggest that the equally distributed quality is broad and metaphysical: we are equal in our common humanity, our worthiness of moral respect.

But all of these qualities either are not distributed equally or are not only distributed equally among people. The argument about pain and pleasure renders all sentient beings as equal, not just persons. 'Humanity' only sharply distinguishes 'humans' if it is reduced to self-consciousness and thus to linguistic capacity, which is not equally distributed. The ability to harm each other and the need to cooperate, whether a consequence or not, includes much more than man: it strengthens the position of the ecologists rather than that of the humanists.

Most egalitarians might say that this search for an ontological meaning of their position is trivial and irrelevant. What matters is not whether there is a sense in which people *are* equal, but the moral superiority of treating them as equal. 'All men are equal' is a rhetorical way of saying that all people should be treated equally. The conventional conservative response to a purely moral statement of egalitarianism is to insist that the costs of equality are too high in terms of other social values. Making people equal educationally can only be achieved by an attack on the family and on personal liberty. Equality of material consumption could only be achieved at the cost of undermining the vast and complex system of incentives which make up the motives of production and thus of reducing, ultimately, the aggregate total of goods and services available.

I do not wish to denigrate the validity of these arguments in the context of particular proposals. But they give away too much. They assume that there is a state, equality, which is, in itself, desirable, and then go on to say that we ought not to attempt to bring it about because it will have so many disadvantages in terms of other desirable states. In this respect, as in many others, conservatism has accepted too many of the premises of its opponents. What is in doubt, and ought to be doubted more often, is whether there is a logically possible state of human equality and whether proposals to make people equal mean anything. Unless there is a positive answer to these questions, the desirability of equality does not arise. I will examine this in terms of three familiar examples in political philosophy, which are: how to make everybody start equally in a running race, how to divide the food in a small community, and how educational resources should be allocated.

The interpretation of equality which is most clear is that of identity of treatment. But this is also the interpretation which has least moral appeal. In distributing food, would anybody seriously recommend that everybody be given the same amount, irrespective of age, appetite, size, nature of work and so on? Surely nobody could believe that because one pupil in the educational system would benefit from the provision of a pair of glasses, all must be given (and made to wear) identical glasses? In the running of races we are, apparently, familiar with something very close to identity of treatment. But this only applies to athletes at a very high and similar level whom we are used to watching in stadia and on television. In most races we distinguish age and sex, those who are disabled in some way have their own events, and in many races there are systems of handicapping.

Thus identity of treatment is, far more often than not, a silly and unacceptable proposal and it is not what people mean when they recommend equality of treatment. Yet, if we retreat from this position and search for an interpretation which makes more moral sense, there is nothing which can be called the egalitarian approach, as such. It is not treating somebody equally to say he must start ten yards behind the others in a race because he is a better runner. A compromise in which he would start five yards behind and still be expected to win, would be merely arbitrary. He is entitled to say that the business of running starts long before the start of a race, that he is a faster runner because he has worked hard to be faster and that the morally significant sense of equality is the equal chance of making oneself into a good runner. In distributing food, given the impropriety of identical treatment, what might count as equal treatment? An equal ratio between size and allocation? Between work (however measured) and amount? Between amount and need (however interpreted)? My purpose here is not to attack these recommendations, but merely to point out that all (and therefore none) can be called the egalitarian approach.

The more complex issues of educational equality illustrate the same point. Identity of treatment is normally ruled out because people have different aptitudes. But what counts as an equal treatment of these different aptitudes? Attempting to get every pupil to the same level in every activity, even if possible, would seem to be as undesirable as treating them identically. Yet allowing them to develop such different aptitudes as they have to an equal extent does not seem possible. Abilities exist in the eye of the beholder or, more generally, in the system of status in society. Mugging old ladies and long-distance spitting are not generally considered worthy of development; football and mathematics are. Even if, by accepting or making a series of value judgements, we can retreat to the position of saying that educational equality consists in the equal right to develop any of a range of approved skills, there is still the problem of the pupil who lacks aptitude generally. It is also apparent that by this standard much that has been done in the name of educational equality is actually drastically inegalitarian in several important senses. Mixed ability teaching in mathematics can have two kinds of inegalitarian consequences. In those schools which do practise it, the good mathematical pupils are disadvantaged by comparison with those of equal potential in those which do not. Even if there were not schools which practised it, such students would be disadvantaged in an important sense provided there still existed activities in which there was a hierarchy of attention based on merit: if football were still organised on the basis of a first team, a second team and so on. Arguably, if one insists that all men are equal (rather than just all Englishmen or all Americans) then such comparisons should only be made for the world as a whole; in this case any attempt to implement educational equality in one country can have important inegalitarian consequences.

The proposal to treat people equally is often interpreted either as a principle of equality of opportunity or as one of relevant differences. The principle of equal opportunity states that, though it is not a proper social objective that everybody should be equal, inequalities can be tolerated only if they are the result of different levels of personal effort and merit and not as the result of different opportunities. The principle is unclear for several reasons, but the greatest of these is the fundamental difficulty of distinguishing between what counts as personal effort and merit and what counts as opportunity. The problem thus duplicates a central difficulty of the concept of liberty.

At one extreme we might take a highly formal notion of the idea of an opporunity, so that it is defined entirely in terms of the rules of the competition. In this sense all children (at least within a given area of local government) had an equal opportunity to go to a grammar school under the 'eleven plus' system in England because all took the same examination on the same day. Entrance to the highest paid government posts is equally open to all. For that matter I have the same opportunity to win the Olympic 1500 metres championship as the current holder of the world record.

This is a sense of equality of opportunity and not one without moral significance. But it is one which simply ignores all the social institutions and their consequences with which egalitarianism is concerned. There is no question that 'social background' affects 'life chances': the income and education of one's parents have a profound effect on how one is likely to do in the eleven plus or entrance to the highest paid government posts. The opposite extreme in the interpretation of equality of opportunity is that which says that all of one's merits, including the personal capacity for directed effort, are the consequences of social circumstances. Thus equality of opportunity, if it means anything at all, means a final equality of achievement between people.

There is no clear and reasonable meaning between these two extremes. Equality of opportunity can only be given substance by taking arbitrary stances on two crucial issues: the kind of evidence which is considered relevant to 'background' as opposed to 'merit' and the time at which opportunity can be said to start. Thus what people generally mean by 'equality of opportunity' is something like 'free compulsory education to the age of 16' or 'the availability of free adult education'. Such prescriptions are the consequences of the other moral and psychological assumptions of the speaker and not logical consequences of the principle of equality of opportunity, which remains purely formal.

It was much easier two or three generations ago to believe that the principle of equality of opportunity meant something clear and substantive. Since then we have had historical experience which suggests that universal suffrage and education plus considerable public ownership of the means of production and redistributive taxation do not create an equal society, as the New Liberals of the late nineteenth and early twentieth centuries had assumed. It is not, or not just, a question of the relationship between nature and nurture; whatever the ultimate limits of genetics, a great deal of educational psychology implies that much of the constraining influence which serves to reduce 'life chances' occurs in the very early years of life and as a consequence of family circumstances. In this context it has become clear that what were once thought of as definitive steps towards equality of opportunity (such as universal free education) now appear to be merely minimal necessary conditions. The proper inference from the evidence of this experience goes beyond concluding that equality of opportunity is difficult to achieve and that we need more crèches and more state nursery schools. The evidence about the formative years in the treatment of a person suggest that it is increasingly difficult to make the principle of equality substantive at all because we have discovered the process which forms the personality is exactly the same as that which serves to limit and define an individual's opportunities.

The conceptual problems of equality of opportunity have important implications for ideas about racial equality. In 'multi-racial' societies like Britain and the United States what we call 'races' are in many cases co-extensive with cultures and sub-cultures. Some of these cultures heavily encourage hard work and intellectual attainment; others do not. To insist, as proponents of affirmative action do, that races must be represented with proportional equality in prestigious or important jobs, is to propose on an aggregate equality of races at the expense of any idea of equal opportunity between individuals. Some members of the previously over-represented race are bound to be deprived of rewards for their merits, and some members of the previously under-represented races are bound to be over-rewarded. This is not necessarily a bad thing, overall; recruiting black policemen at the expense of better qualified whites may be a good utilitarian policy in a multi-racial society. But, in a very important sense, it is the opposite of equality of opportunity.

The hard, formal sense of equality of opportunity has logical and moral advantages. It is, at least, clear what counts as an opportunity in this sense. And, for all the weight of sociological evidence about factors affecting people's life chances, there is no evidence of determinism. To talk of life chances is to talk of probabilities, not certainties; for all the improbability of people taking opportunities, they can still be said to have them. An illegitimate boy from Lossiemouth did become Prime Minister of Great Britain, however improbable it was that he should do so. To emphasise constantly the improbability of people from certain kinds of background achieving very much is likely to undermine their morale and motivation. There is something to be said for the view that opportunity, like many other social phenomena, is best regarded as a self-fulfilling prophecy.

It is even more difficult to draw substantial implications from the principle of relevant differences. In its general form this states that people should be treated equally unless there are differences between them relevant to their treatment and therefore good reasons for treating them differently. It hardly takes a sophisticated philosopher to spot that any substantive interpretation of this version of the principle of equality must depend on what is allowed as a relevant difference or a good reason. Almost any general social value might be allowed and it would be very difficult to exclude utility: broadly, the form of the argument would be that people ought to be treated differently in a particular respect because it would be in the interest of society as a whole to do so. For instance, it might be argued that policemen should be paid considerably more than other workers because of the benefits of attracting good applicants to the police force. (The same recommendation could, of course, be derived from several different political values or principles.)

Any principle of relevant differences which ignored utilitarian arguments would be morally implausible: the principle that we should never treat people differently in order to benefit the whole could not be held by a rational person: the most obvious examples which refute it are those of shipwrecks and balloons, where all might die unless one is sacrificed. Or, at least, we could allow Rawls's principle that people can be privileged provided *everybody* (and not merely the aggregate of everybody) benefits. But having allowed either of these principles, anything is possible. It is a matter of judgement to decide which differences between the sexes, for example, are in the interests of everybody. Apartheid in South Africa is justified precisely by a theory of relevant differences which suggests that the separate (but equal) development of national cultures is in the interests of the majority of people in the Union.

The example of apartheid may well seem a *reductio ad absurdum* in the context of a discussion of equality. It also exemplifies a general feature of the structure of arguments which justify social systems: real inequalities are said to be necessary conditions of the higher equality which is an essential feature of the society. The great differences of wealth in capitalism are justified by a fundamental equality of political rights and economic freedom. The privileged position of party members in Marxist-Leninist states is necessary to achieve the final equality of communism. Many forms of Christian conservatism have mirrored this argument: equality before God justifies and renders trivial the inequalities which God sanctions on earth. In short, the concept of equality of treatment is wholly incoherent. It means nothing; it tells us nothing; it is part of the justificatory rhetoric of politics and is not a moral value which can be taken seriously. So egalitarianism is not a position which conservatives should oppose: it is not a position at all.

But this does not mean that egalitarians are saying nothing. For the most part, in specific arguments, egalitarians are attacking particular inequalities and recommending their abolition. The typical egalitarian position in a practical argument is not 'all men are equal' or 'all men should be treated equally', but 'x, y and z are inequalities which should be removed.' But why should they be removed? 'Because they are inequalities' would be the strictly egalitarian reply, but this cannot be the true reason. To that reason the conservative could always reply, 'But why those inequalities?' or, 'So is the alternative you are suggesting.' Reasons for recommending the abolition of inequalities can draw on many values and principles; a common form of argument is utilitarian, that the inequalities involve a waste of human potential. But more typically the justification resorts to ideas of fairness and justice: the practice is judged to be unfair, incompatible with justice.

Thus egalitarian arguments collapse and blur into arguments about fairness and justice. But what is justice? David Miller in *Social Justice* suggests that 'the most valuable general definition of justice is that which brings out its distributive character most plainly: justice is *suum cuique*, to each his due.' There are, though, as Miller stresses, very different kinds of criteria which suggest not merely alternative answers to the question of what is due to us, but even opposite ones. There is our due in the sense of the satisfaction of our needs, our due in the sense of a reward appropriate to the merit we have shown and our due defined as the practical acknowledgement of our rights.

The idea of merit presupposes a set of standards and the rules of an implied competition or game. There can, of course, be many such standards and many different sets of rules. The idea of need also presupposes standards: needs for what? as defined by whom?

We have no intransitive needs: we can always die. As Sidney Smith said to the satirist who said that he needed to live: 'I fail to see why.' Even if we say that 'needs' can be ordinarily taken to mean 'needs for living', there are very few of these and the content of justice in this sense is very small. And there are, as we have seen, many ways of talking about rights.

Thus the idea of justice covers at least three widely different and even opposing ideas. Each is open to a large variety of evaluative interpretations and can be applied in different ways to rules, practices, people and individual decisions. There is little in common (to use Miller's examples) between the accounts of justice given by such articulate theorists as Hume, Spencer and Kroptokin and this is not to take into account less respectable ideas like the Nazi conception of racial justice and many people's 'burning', though often inarticulate, sense of injustice.

The existence, in most human minds, of a potentially powerful sense of justice is something of enormous importance in practical politics, but it has little theoretical content. For the most part, the sense of injustice is narrowly blinkered. As philosophers from Montesquieu to Spencer and many twentieth-century sociologists have pointed out, most people's sense of injustice is more dependent on particular expectations than it is on generally applicable concepts. A particular sense of justice depends on a particular comparative reference group. In other words, if we are to understand a man's sense of justice and injustice and how it may move him we need to know what he expects from life (including what he believes to be the rules that govern the social game) and with whom he compares himself. A major may feel an overwhelming sense of injustice because he has not been made a colonel. This sense is based on his comparison with a man who is a colonel whom he believes to be idle and without great talent. It is likely to be vastly inflated by his having been led to believe that he would be made a colonel. He does not consider the argument that by some standards he is very fortunate to be an officer at all. Thus it is with boilermakers and riveters and the whole 'leap-frogging' structure of British wage negotiation: it is a change of position in respect of one's traditional rivals which informs most people's sense of injustice and not any generally applicable ideas about distribution. Paradoxically, 'fairer' systems of distribution by broad standards can lead to greater senses of injustice by changing people's expectations and reference groups so that, for instance, miners begin to compare themselves with stock-brokers, or nurses seek a reward for their job which is commensurate with its importance and difficulty – something which, if taken seriously, they could not possibly be paid.

An ordinary sense of justice is often based on sentiments which cannot be elevated into theories. Theories of justice are based on different and even opposing criteria which are themselves subject to widely varying interpretation. Justice means everything and nothing in the context of the distribution of social and material goods. Suppose somebody demands 'Is it fair or just that some people are starving and some unemployed while others have large private incomes?' The only reasonable answer can be, 'According to some well-established standards, yes. According to rival and alternative standards, no.' There are standards by which it is quite unfair that the state should prevent a man from giving his wealth to his children and hand out money to those who have done nothing to deserve it and standards which imply the opposite of both these propositions.

It is no exaggeration to say that the principle 'all men should be treated equally' means nothing while that 'all men should be treated justly' can be used to mean almost anything.

7

RIGHTS

Rights are a very important and broad category of human relations. It would be difficult either to act within a society or to talk about a society without using the concept of rights. It would not be impossible, though: all talk of rights could be translated into talk of laws, rules, conventions, roles and moral judgement, though such talk would be clumsier and lack the rhetorical power of talking about rights. Statements about rights describe important dimensions of any human relationship, those which involve claims and expectations and have implications for rules, laws and moral judgements. Broadly and simply, people's rights are what they are allowed to do.

The logic of the concept of rights is that statements about rights imply statement about duties. Very often this connection is misunderstood. The only direct, logical inference about duties which can be made from statements about x's rights is about the duties of other people to acknowledge those rights. If x has the right to say what he likes, then other people have a duty to allow him to speak. If we can't say that they have that duty, then there is no significant sense in which he has that right.

But the observation that rights imply duties is very often taken to mean that the right-holder has duties simply by virtue of having rights. This is not necessarily true: that x has the right to say what he wants does not imply that he has a duty to say reasonable things or to support or accept the right of others to say what they want nor anything else. It may be legal and a very good thing (depending on the circumstances and one's point of view) that x and only x can say what he wants. Having a right does not, in itself, imply that one has any kind of duty.

There are several reasons for the confusion. The first is that, over the years, there has been so much pious talk about the duties which go with rights (and privileges) that it is easy for the unquestioning to fall into the assumption that the relationship is a necessary one. Prefects, district commissioners, those with money and so on are frequently said to have onerous duties as a consequence of their rights. But the statement of consequence is a value judgement; it says only that those with rights ought to behave in certain ways. In no way is it a logical implication of the meaning of rights, as the relation between x's rights and other people's duties is.

Many rights are distributed conditionally upon the performance of duties: the perks and the stipend go with the job. If one does the job, one has a right to the benefits. If one ceases to perform the duty one may, in some circumstances, automatically forfeit the rights. But not all rights are in fact conditional and none are *necessarily* so. Many kinds of property rights (such as ownership of shares and money) are not conditional in any real sense.

The variety of rights is enormous. There are hundreds of sub-categories into which rights can be divided and dozens of distinctions which can be drawn between types of rights. There are prescriptive rights which are 'laid down' in some way or other and residual rights which exist because nobody has a right to prevent or interfere. There is the familiar distinction between 'de jure' and 'de facto' rights. The broad category contains several large and important categories within it. There are the rights to command and direct other people: authority, in other words. Then there are property rights to use, exclude, transfer, share (and so on) physical objects. The range and complexity of rights of use, including mast and tillage and rights of way, for instance, is quite enormous. But there is a more fundamental distinction in dealing with rights than any distinctions between the types and sub-types of right. There are quite separate ways of talking about rights, different ontological levels at which rights can be assumed, claimed or stated. At least four different levels must be distinguished.

Positive-legal

At this level a statement about rights is about an existing system of law. If I say 'I have a right to keep any money I make in fees and royalties', the most frequent way I might be contradicted would be by somebody quoting a Finance Act or similar statute and saying 'No, you don't. You are liable for tax under the following section. . . '. In other words, one of the ways we can talk about rights is a morally neutral way of talking about what the law says. This is not to say that we can always (or even often) make statements about rights which are facts. There is a disagreement about what the law is, both about its general nature and particular content. Broadly, it is a system of rules enforced by sovereign bodies operating within territorial limits. But the system can be highly unsystematic, the rules are often ambiguous and sometimes contradictory, sovereignty is disputed and cases cannot always be confined to neat territorial limits.

There are two great objections to treating statements about the law as facts. The first is that laws not only contain, but inevitably contain, terms such as 'the public interest', 'material advantage' and 'reasonable excuse' (to take three which occur in the Prevention of Terrorism Act, 1976). These terms cannot be interpreted and the laws made to mean anything, without the introduction of value judgements. The second is that the process of making and changing the law is also, in part, the process of deciding what it contains. Whether or not my fees and royalties are taxable (given, say, the place in which I claim to be resident or the expenses I have incurred in earning them) may be more like a matter of conjecture and speculation than one of fact. Nevertheless the positive legal way of talking about rights is relatively factual and neutral. We can go to a solicitor or citizens' adviser to find out what our rights are in a particular matter. It may be that they can offer us only interpretation or prediction, but this does not make the talk of rights any less true or neutral than other fields of social discourse.

Positive-sociological

Statements about rights are often not about the law, but about beliefs, values, conventions and practices which lie outside the law. Many kinds of gambling debt and work practice are not recognised by the law. In England the right to pick brambles or to park on the public highway in front of one's own home are not part of the law. Within marriage or friendship we would often claim to have a right to consideration or to information. These claims are not (or not only) prescriptions of what the law ought to be, or a rhetorical device for saying that the speaker shoud be treated better. They are appeals to allocative standards which exist in the minds of most people or normal people or reasonable people. If we say 'Look, I've worked here ten years, I think I have a right to be consulted about any major changes . . .' or 'I am your father – I have a right to know if you are in trouble' then we are not fundamentally interested in the law, but in standards which can be said to exist in the same way as the law does but independently of it.

The boundary between these standards and the law is an extremely complex one; there are many shifts and disputed areas. Suppose I park outside a house, ignoring a board which says POLITE NOTICE. NO PARKING. The owner of the house comes to remonstrate with me. He has a right to park outside his own house, he says. I tell him that his 'right' is a wooden lie, a piece of legal mythology. He says that the law is nothing to do with it, he still has a right and that he also has a desperate need because he often has to dash off to his work at a moment's notice. He is not necessarily making any prescription about what the law ought to say; it may be that there are insuperable difficulties preventing the establishment of a legal right to park in front of one's own home and that he fully recognises them.

In a sense, I am right and he is wrong. The 'harder', more formal way of talking about rights does not give him the right he claims. But in another sense, many people might take the view that he is right and that I am being bloody-minded. The law itself might recognise that sense by regarding my attitude as provocative. Extra-legal standards inform the law and are sometimes incorporated into the law. On occasions they contradict the law and many people would take the view that the law is 'an ass' on these occasions. Equally the law can undermine or change extra-legal standards; legal prohibitions on racial discrimination and intolerance appear to have changed extra-legal standards in a number of countries (and perhaps achieved the reverse in a number of other cases). But, for all the intimacy and complexity of the causal relationship between the law and extra-legal standards, they remain quite separate and distinguishable entities. They provide separate ways of talking about rights.

Critical standards

One difficult ambiguity about 'rights' is that any statement about rights can have both 'is' and 'ought' implications. 'I have a right to x' can mean 'My right to x exists' or 'My right to x ought to exist.' It can also combine the two by appealing either to a legal standard or to a non-legal social standard in a way which presupposes and solicits moral approval of the standard.

But there is an esablished usage of rights which makes no such appeal: in which 'I have a right to x' is quite compatible with the acceptance that neither the law nor a widely shared morality contains this right. It implies only that I *ought* to be treated as if I had the right. Positivist and utilitarian philosophers since Bentham have condemned this way of talking and insisted that we must distinguish clearly between the existence of an entity and the belief that it ought to exist. But however reasonable their arguments, convention and rhetorical value are against them; stating a right is the principle way of claiming, creating or establishing such a right.

Natural rights

'Natural' rights are those which can be said to belong to all persons in all societies. It follows that they are not conditional and can be said to be 'inalienable' and 'imprescriptable'. In contemporary argument they are more commonly referred to as 'human' rights, though historically the debate has taken place in terms of 'natural' rights. Whether there is anything which can properly be said to fall into this category is the central question about rights in political philosophy.

The variety of senses of 'right' lends a bewildering complexity to arguments about rights, which is complicated even further by the different levels or statuses of talk about rights. This complexity exists across the wide family of 'rights' concepts and explains, for instance, the force of 'property is theft.' But a simpler example is perhaps better in explaining how argument can work. Suppose I am standing on the pavement of a street in England early on a Saturday morning talking to a friend. The street is a shopping street, but it is early in the morning and there are very few people about. A policeman comes up and tells me to move along. I might reply that I have a right to stand on the pavement. (I might well add 'if I want to', but this is quite redundant and I would have the right or not

have it irrespective of any desire to exercise it.) The policeman
might then say that I don't have such a right, that it has been
established in English law that standing on a pavement without
making progress along it constitutes a crime, that of obstruction.
But that, I might say to the policeman, though true, is utterly
trivial. The law he is referring to is one which is enforced in some
tiny fraction of one per cent of cases and nobody in his right mind
could think it applicable in these circumstances. I might threaten
him with the attitude to his attitude which might be taken by his
sergeant or a jury or British television audiences. Alternatively, I
might make an appeal to his critical judgement of whether he is
doing right in treating me as if I do not have a right, irrespective of
what any third parties might say or do. 'Surely I have a right to
stand here quietly?' I might demand. At the most grandiose I might
say that whatever English judges, juries or policemen might say, I
was a human being and as such had a natural right to go about my
own business.

ARE THERE ANY NATURAL RIGHTS?

The question of whether or not there are any natural rights, in the
sense of rights which belong to all human beings at all times, falls
into two parts. There is the ontological question of whether such
rights can be said to exist and, if so, in what sense. Then there is the
moral question which asks, irrespective of the actual existence of
such rights, whether we should act as if they exist. The two questions
can be connected, of course, by self-fulfilment.

The ontological question is relatively trivial, but its answer is
quite clear: there is no proper sense in which rights belonging to all
human beings can be said to exist. Rights can be said to exist only in
the context of a legal or social system. To talk of rights critically is
not to assert their existence, but to state what ought to exist or how
we ought to act. There are no rights whose existence is embodied in
all legal or social standards; they would be hardly worth discussing
if there were. More accurately, there are no such rights which have
any substance. It is true that almost all codes of law and morality
condemn theft and murder, but these are mere formalities: what
sort of killing you can do, and how you may take possession of
material objects, are questions which are answered very differently

in different codes. To say that everybody has a right to their own property or a right to live, is no different from saying that everybody has a right to be treated well.

The moral question is much more important. Are there any rights which we ought to assume that people have in all circumstances? There is no shortage of sources from which candidates can be quoted: sources include the revolutionary principles of the French and American republics set up in the eighteenth century, the United Nations Declaration of Human Rights of 1948, and a hundred other charters, declarations and constitutions. For the most part these statements of rights contain pious generalities, incapable of being taken substantively. Tom Paine in *The Rights of Man*, for instance, said that 'The end of all political associations is the preservation of the natural and imprescriptable rights of man: These rights are Liberty, Property, Security and the right to resist oppression.'

None of these expressions means anything substantive. Liberty and property will be discussed later in this book (see chapters 8 and 9), but what could a right to security or to life consist of? It could not mean that the state guarantees to protect its citizens from all dangers, diseases and attacks which might kill them: no state could guarantee to do that. Indeed, in practice, all modern states must carefully cost the lives of their citizens. Their documents regularly contain statements of the form 'This piece of medical equipment costs x million pounds and will save y lives, so we cannot afford it' or 'This road safety procedure costs z thousand pounds and will save n lives, so it is not worth investment.'

It might be thought that a right to life or security might at least guarantee that the state would refrain from killing its own citizens. But it has rarely been interpreted in that way: the French and American republics have been at the forefront of the practice of execution. They have tended to treat Liberty in the same way, tolerating the freedom to express opinions except that they take it as obvious that this does not extend to activities which are un-American or contrary to the integrity of the French state, or obscene, the expression of opinion in most cases counting as an activity. In any case, there is only a fine and trivial distinction between the state killing people in the form of execution and its regular practice of shortening their lives through its medical, economic, transport and foreign policies. As far as the victim is concerned there may only be a formal difference between being killed by the state and being

killed by other agencies because of the state's negligence or incompetence in policing (*perhaps* complemented by an inadequate system
of punishment). In short, all the traditional 'natural' or 'human'
rights seem so vague and general that anything and nothing can be
made of them and, consequently, horrific crimes can be committed
in their name, as Madame de Staël put it.

The conservative attack on natural rights has consistently emphasised both the semantic and ontological weakness of claims about
rights and the dangerous consequences of such loose and general
claims. Most famously and passionately, Jeremy Bentham wrote in
his *Anarchical Fallacies*, 'That which has no existence cannot be
destroyed – that which cannot be destroyed cannot require anything
to preserve it from destruction. Natural rights is simple nonsense:
natural and prescriptable rights rhetorical nonsense – nonsense upon
stilts.' Similarly, Edmund Burke, in *Reflections on the Revolution in
France*: 'far is my heart from witholding in practice . . . the *real* rights
of men. In denying their false claims of right I do not mean to injure
those which are real and such as their pretended rights would totally
destroy.'

The condemnations of natural rights which Burke and Bentham
put forward are, paradoxically, very similar, but founded on almost
opposite premises. Both assert that 'natural rights' is a piece of
ontological nonsense and that real rights can only exist in a particular
social and legal context. Both are keen to add that such nonsense is
not by any means harmless; it can cause enormous destruction to
valuable social institutions. But they make opposite assumptions
about the human capacity to plan rationally. Burke's position is that
this capacity is very low indeed: we must be guided by the wisdom
inherent in the complex network of contracts and arrangements
which already exists in society. Natural rights are dangerous because
they threaten these arrangements: 'Against them there can be no
prescription; against them no argument is binding: they admit no
temperament and no compromise; anything witheld from their full
demand is so much fraud and injustice. Against them let no government look for security in the length of its continuance or in the
justice and levity of its administration.'

Conversely, Bentham assumed a very large capacity for rational
planning based on calculations of the maximum benefit for society
as a whole of any law or policy. Given this assumption any outside
constraints, like natural law or natural rights, or legislators' purpose

in organising the best possible lives for their citizens, were unacceptable. There could be no good reason for any such generality:
'as there is no right which ought not to be maintained so long as it is
on the whole advantageous to the society that it should be maintained, so there is no right which, when the abolition of it is
advantageous to society, should not be abolished.' Bentham's pol-
emics reached heights of venom in describing natural rights: 'from
real laws come real rights; but from imaginary laws, from laws of
nature, fancied and invented by poets, rhetoricians and dealers in
moral and intellectual poisons, come imaginary rights, a bastard
brood of monsters. . . .'

The two sets of arguments against rights are very similar, for all
the wideness of this gap in assumptions. Both consider that the
doctrine of natural rights is a threat to established, proper and useful
ways of doing things. For both, the fundamental basis is utilitarian:
it is the quality of the effects of our policies and practices which
matters in the end. That Burke is a 'blinded' utilitarian who thinks
we must always be carefully guided by custom in judging these
effects, and Bentham a rationalist, who thinks they can be accurately
calculated by sound legislators, is of little importance in this argument. The critical case against rights is based on the same conservative judgements, and these need further investigation.

The argument can be put as a dichotomy. Either the doctrine of
natural rights is empty of moral substance or it implies prescriptions
for conduct. In the former case the emphasis must be on 'nonsense'
rather than 'dangerous', but it can be argued that, empty as it is, the
doctrine has been used as the rhetorical justification for many kinds
of bad government. However, if the doctrine actually implies forms
of conduct, then it must lead to our acting in ways contrary to our
normal moral judgement, and judgement is a sounder basis for
action than abstract principles.

To follow the latter course of argument it is necessary to find
more plausible candidates than the loose and promiscuous notions
of liberty and security. Two candidates emerge from modern debate
which do appear to be much more precise: the right to work and the
right not to be tortured. The apparent precision of the former is
illusory. What is meant by 'work' or a 'job'? Doing something
productive? What counts as production? Arguably, it is more productive to sit at home and make cups of tea for one's mother than to
waste resources by producing coal and steel which nobody wants.

The same problems apply to 'useful'. In any case most people do not include voluntary work when they talk of the right to work. They mean paid work. But how much pay counts as a wage? The market would ensure that everybody had 'work' provided they priced themselves low enough. So the 'right to work' must mean the right to be paid above a certain level. At what level? A level just above biological poverty? This level is very difficult to define, and whatever the definition, resources may not be sufficient. The level of poverty as defined by the expectations of a particular society? That may do irreparable harm to the economy of that society by wasting its resources, inflating its currency and trapping many people into 'work' which exists only because of an abstract principle of 'work' and not because of any effective demand for their services. It would be exactly what Bentham meant by 'rhetorical nonsense – nonsense upon stilts'.

'Torture' would seem to be easier to define than 'work'. It is the use of severe pain or mental distress for the purposes of punishment or obtaining information. This is not really precise, but let us suppose that it is; at least, there are cases which would be so widely agreed to be torture that there could be no serious controversy about the use of the word. Giving severe electric shocks to the genitals of men or women for the purpose of extracting confessions from them is clearly torture and it is repulsive behaviour. But this is not to say that there can be an absolute right not to be tortured. Is it wrong, if you have in your capture a known planter of bombs in populous places, to inflict severe pain on him to coerce him to tell you where his bombs are or who his companions are? Very basic instincts and judgements suggest it would be right to torture: not just the idea of utility, but also an instinct of fairness. It would be quite wrong to treat the planter of bombs as if he were to be protected from the kind of pain and mutilation which he inflicts on other people. Yet we would have to exclude him if we are to 'take rights seriously', as Professor Ronald Dworkin puts it.

To oppose the idea of a natural right to work or not to be tortured is just that, opposition to an abstract and general principle. It does not mean that one is committed to increasing unemployment or to toasting burglars over red-hot fires to find out who their associates are. There are powerful arguments against torture: it is cruel and disgusting; it corrupts the torturer; it intensifies political and military conflicts; it is difficult to draw the line. Some might judge that they could scarcely envisage the circumstances in which it would be right to do it. For that matter, it is a good idea for governments to offer citizens the opportunity of useful and remunerative work. But no good can come of asserting a universal right in either respect, and considerable harm might result.

The European Court of Human Rights has declared, in effect, that caning is a form of torture. In some cases caning may be administered sadistically or it may have more bad consequences than good. But in other contexts it may be a necessary part of an ordered and efficient educational institution. The powerful arguments against clear cases of torture are misplaced when applied to caning: it is often done paternally, by decent people who can draw a clear line between corporal punishment and genuine harm or cruelty; it does not normally intensify conflict and it is compatible with the joint acceptance of rules by the actor and the recipient. It is absurd to equate caning with torture, but a prohibition on caning is exactly the kind of absurdity which is likely to result from the replacement of complex moral judgements about punishment by bogus theoretical calculations about rights.

The single paragraph of abstract principle which has probably done more harm to more people than any other is the fifth amendment of the constitution of the United States of America. This says:

No person shall be held to answer for a capital, or otherwise infamous crime, unless on a presentment or indictment of a grand jury, except in cases arising in the land or naval forces, or in the militia, when in actual service in time of war or public danger; nor shall any person be subject for the same offense to be twice put in jeopardy of life or limb; nor shall be compelled in any criminal case to be a witness against himself, nor be deprived of life, liberty or property, without due process of law; nor shall private property be taken for public use, without just compensation.

This has been interpreted to imply (among many other things) that extensive public control of private real estate cannot be allowed in the United States. What this means in Northern California, for example, is that nobody can prevent the development of a huge strip-conurbation stretching from San Francisco to San Jose. People do not want this conurbation and it threatens the long-term ecological and economic interests of the vast majority, but the rights of the owners of real estate are allowed to prevail.

The same amendment also allows wrongdoers a vast array of methods of avoiding conviction. The most ridiculous and unjust of these in my mind is that in some circumstances conviction cannot occur if the arresting authority has used improper procedures. It is not merely the *content* of the fifth amendment which poses problems. To enshrine any set of abstract principles as the basis of one's law and government means that society is perpetually bound by a set of words and a set of procedures for interpreting those words in particular cases. It follows that there must be contests for the favourable interpretation of crucial words. These contests must be won by those with the most resources (and therefore the best lawyers). It is the wealthy whose will prevails against that of the people in Northern California; it is the Mafia who stay out of gaol. The possibilities of interpretation can be boundless: liberty is compatible with slavery, but not with the control of hand guns. Abstract and absolute rights are, in practice, a licence for gangsterism and the worst excesses of capitalism.

Human rights have even less place in application to foreign policy. What does one do about regimes which do not acknowledge them? Refuse to trade and impoverish the people who are the very victims? Jimmy Carter refused support for the Shah of Iran on the grounds that his regime did not properly respect human rights. Nor did it, by the standard of a wide variety of declarations and theories of human rights. But the withdrawal of American support was instrumental in bringing about the collapse of the Shah's government and its replacement by an 'Islamic' regime, a regime which was in many respects far worse, a regime which sanctioned people being buried to their necks in sand and stoned to death, and women being treated as domestic animals. Absolute principles do not make good politics; morally speaking, they can lift you out of the frying pan and into the fire.

Some might argue that I have taken rights too seriously, that a natural right does not imply any rigid and absolute rule, but merely one of guidance, to be taken into account like a legal principle. But this is the weakest interpretation of all, not so much nonsense on stilts as nonsense with holes in it: 'Yes, it is your right, but you can't have it in these circumstances because I have reasons for not conceding it.'

8

PROPERTY AND OWNERSHIP

Property rights relate people to objects, usually to the use and usefulness of the object. Talking about property rights is one of the most fundamental ways of talking about social arrangements and also one of the broadest ways of talking about right and wrong.

There can be a very wide variety of property rights within one society. In England, rights of way and access allow people to cross and enter land; a modern addition, membership of the National Trust, allows those who have it access to certain places of interest. Many kinds of grazing rights allow the use of land for feeding animals; 'mast', the right of grazing pigs in beech woods, is still held by a few individuals. Tenancy can confer a very variable bundle of rights upon individuals, ranging from a very limited and arbitrarily terminable right of use to the fairly full rights of possession, use, management and security which the law gives to many people who rent houses (whether from private landlords or public authorities). There are many ways in which one can share an interest in some-thing, ranging from the informality of a shared allotment to the highly formal arrangements for holding shares in a public company and their voting rights and rights to information.

These constitute a very small selection of the kinds of property rights which can exist. For the most part, talking about them is talking about the law, about what it says and about what its judiciary is likely to say in specified circumstances. But some of them just exist in our moral assumptions, with the law just a vague back-ground of ill-defined relevance. My neighbour may have no status in law in respect of his half of the allotment, if it is in my name. There are many rules governing gambling or one's place in a queue or the collection of wild fruit or the possession of objects found which are independent of the law or even contradictory to it.

Just as there are many kinds of property rights within a society, there can be great differences between the kinds of arrangement and distribution of property right between different societies. But a society without property rights is not conceivable. We could only say that there were no property rights if there were no rules about the possession and use of objects. If one was bound only by whim as to which buildings one entered, which bed one slept in, which fruit one picked and which underwear one wore, we could say that there were no property rights. But such an absence of arrangements could not reasonably be called a society at all. Communal property is quite different from non-property; it involves the necessity of rules governing membership of the community and also rights of use. These rights of use may be based on seniority or need or priority (queueing and 'finders keepers'). Or they may be based on labour, entitling people to the produce of their own picking or tilling or fishing or hunting. The basis of these rules may vary considerably, but the community cannot be said to exist unless there are rules about the use of objects and thus property rights.

It is not merely improbable that a society could exist without a system of property rights; it is inconceivable. Property rights cannot be sharply distinguished from the most fundamental and essential of personal rights. Some, such as rights over clothes, beds and toothbrushes, for instance, are indistinguishable from rights of privacy and personal security. The more complex case of overlap is with the right to the products of one's own labour. In this case, too, the right to be a person with some kind of autonomy seems very close to the idea of having a right to use and possess one's own creations. 'It's mine . . . I found it, I made it, I grew it' is a very common and intuitive form of moral inference, so much so that virtually all political theorists accept some form of a labour theory of property. That one's own products should be one's own is agreed by Locke and Marx, though interpreted in very different ways.

However, like so much in political theory, this principle of rights turns out to be an empty formality. In the first place, there is the complication of joint labour: most artefacts are produced by several different stages, some of which necessarily require more than one person's labour. Coal has to be cut and transported, bagged and delivered. It is not a question of one person's labour contributing this or that proportion of the final product; each stage and activity is a necessary condition of useful production. Most production also involves the 'mixing' of labour with goods, both fixed capital goods and recurrently produced goods. These were, in almost every case, created, maintained, preserved, organised and put in the right place at the right time by someone's labour. In a monetary system with private capital a very large element of production can be said to be the provision of capital which can make men tens or thousands of times or even infinitely more productive than they would be with their own hands. How can the organisation of capital be compared with other labour? Then there is the question of the circumstances under which one can sell one's labour (or its product, from which it may be indistinguishable in economic terms). Crudely, labour can be sold under very favourable or very unfavourable terms depending on the principles and arrangements in the society.

The right to the product of one's own labour seems to have some precision if applied to a lone gatherer in an abundant wilderness who can be said to have no duties or responsibilities. But introduce cooperation, society and its rights, or capital and it becomes all but meaningless. Coal miners do not produce coal; they cut it. Geologists, architects, engineers, accountants, administrators, advertisers and lorry drivers, among others, turn this organic refuse into something useful and valued. Nor does it make sense to estimate what part of the coal the miners 'produce'. We can safely say that some of it is their produce (though this is a dubious principle to apply in a monetary system when their activities are making a loss), but it makes no more sense to say how much their labour is worth than it would to give a figure for the relative usefulness of the engine and the wheels of a car. Thus 'labour' theories of property, value and reward are widely accepted but empty. Substantively, anything can be made from the formal principle that a man is entitled to the product of his own labour. It can be, and has been, used as the basis of Lockean justifications of capitalism and Marxian justifications of socialism.

OWNERSHIP

If 'property' is taken to mean 'property rights' in the sense that I have discussed them and in which they are generally discussed by lawyers and political theorists, then it is logically impossible to be 'against' property as such; it is only possible to be against particular systems of property rights. But this is a technical sense. Ordinarily, when people talk about 'other people's property' or estate agents refer to 'the property' or (a more complex case) notices pronounce that something is 'public property', they are referring either to a relation of ownership or to an object owned. Ownership is a particular arrangement of property rights; it is unfortunate (if clarity is the objective) that 'property' and 'ownership' are used so loosely and interchangeably.

The confusion is more complete in French; *proprieté* means both ownership and property as in the expression *pleine proprieté*, meaning freehold ownership. Proudhon asked himself 'What is property?' and replied that it was 'theft'. That, at least, is the usual translation, but it would make more sense to say that 'ownership is theft'. There are several senses of property, including the broadest sense of the whole range of rights over objects, in which one could not coherently say that 'property' was theft. To complete this complex and tortuous triangle of words one must add that possession, the actual control of objects, is only contingently related to property and ownership.

A classic modern account of the 'full liberal model' of ownership is given by A. M. Honoré in his essay, 'Ownership'. In this account, owning something consists in a range of 'incidents'. Most of these are rights: to possess, to use, to manage, to lend, to transfer, to exclude, to destroy, rights to the income and to security (or 'absence of term'). Ownership also denotes duties and liabilities, including execution and thus the possibility of confiscation to pay off the owner's debts, the prohibition of harmful uses and a liability for the consequences of the state or use of the thing owned, so that owners can be subjected to civil liability or, in some circumstances, criminal prosecution, if their cars, animals or buildings cause harm to others.

The 'full liberal model' of ownership represents a paradigm or ideal type which, though frequently realised in practice, is not fully realised in many of the most important and interesting cases which we would normally call ownership. If you own land or buildings in England you are subject to the Town and Country Planning Acts which, since 1947, have allotted the development rights of land and buildings to the state. Your right to use the property is confined to its existing use; any change of use must be sanctioned by a local planning authority and/or the Secretary of State for the Department of the Environment. This has important implications for the right to manage. The right to income is subject to taxation, as is the right to transfer, often heavily so in the case of legacies. The right to exclude may be severely limited by the existence and the rights of sitting tenants, by rights of way and access and by the absence of a criminal law of trespass and the consequent possibilities for squatting. All of these possibilities severely limit and may even eradicate the right to possess. The right to destroy is subject to development control and is very difficult to recover in the case of 'listed' buildings or those in special areas such as conservation areas.

These arrangements in English law are a fairly extreme case of the weakening of ownership, though many of them are duplicated in different parts of Europe. They rarely weaken the duties and liabilities of ownership. The American ownership of real estate, by contrast, is much closer to the Honoré paradigm.

A further complication to the concept of ownership is that large and important entities are often owned not by persons as such, but by collective, abstract or even fictional entities, typically by institutions. These can include firms, churches, states, local authorities and more general collective entities such as the 'public' and the 'community'. In some cases the full liberal model of ownership works reasonably clearly for such institutions: the institution exists as a system of authority which delegates and distributes the rights of ownership which it holds as a (fictional) individual. Thus a college or university may leave the question of access to its sports grounds and pavilions to a committee, which in turn, entrusts them to a head groundsman. Or a local authority may define very carefully the occasions and terms on which people can possess and use the books in its libraries. But even where it is relatively clear that the rights of ownership exist and that the institutions are capable of controlling and distributing them, there remains a paradox that the 'owners' can be the recipients of very few of the rights. One of the consequences of what James Burnham called 'the divorce between ownership and control' is that shareholders in modern public companies have virtually none of the rights of ownership: they can no more walk in and out of factories nor repossess machinery than non-shareholders can. Their rights are to vote on certain occasions and to be informed in certain ways. The rights which go to make up ownership are actually controlled by a structure of authority within the firm which may well be under the command of persons who are not owners at all.

There are some cases where the possession of and authority over the rights of ownership is so obscure that it may be less misleading to say that the entities are not owned at all. The most difficult cases are those of 'public', 'national' or 'state' ownership. Who can lend or transfer the land owned by British nationalised industries? Does anyone possess or can anyone destroy state monuments? There may be grounds for excluding people from public parks, but they are rarely connected with membership of the relevant 'public'. In some cases of public ownership the authority over the rights of ownership is so diffuse that it is misleading to say these rights exist at all and thus that the thing is owned in any proper sense.

For much of western history, ownership has been a fairly unclear concept because major assets have been communally, feudally or ecclesiastically owned. Private ownership (in its clear and strong sense) of the major means of production is a relatively distinctive phenomenon associated with what can loosely be called 'early capitalism', and its proponents would argue that it has demonstrated by far the most productive capacity of any form of authority over objects. Nevertheless, no sooner was it established than it was weakened in many societies. Not only was it weakened by the kind of reinstitutionalisation which followed the invention of limited liability, but also by the general strengthening of the state's role. The 'divorce between ownership and control' has also been accompanied by a division of the actual rights of ownership. This is most clearly exemplified by the nationalisation of development rights in England which I have already discussed. But it is also implicit in the fiscal and management arrangements of modern states and the eternal possibility that assets may be nationalised.

The important questions about property are about ownership. They are: What kind of things should the state allow to be owned? and, What kind of ownership should it allow? Initially, at least, we can arrange opinion on what can be owned along a continuum. At one end of the line are kinds of goods the full liberal ownership of which is endorsed by almost everybody; such intimate items as underwear and toothbrushes where the case for private ownership seems primarily hygienic. At the other end are the resources of order and security, tanks, fighter planes and nuclear bombs, objects of such power and destruction that it would be difficult to conceive of a case for private ownership. Along the continuum are a number of points which can be seen as significant moral landmarks, points indicated by such questions as: Can people own land? Can they own the 'means of production'? Can they own enough productive capacity to employ other men? Can they own enough to live without working themselves?

A continuum needs a numerical variable to relate its points. The obvious candidate in this case would be the value of the goods which can be owned in a monetary and market system, whether real or hypothetical. This does not capture the full subtleties of the morally significant questions, but it has to suffice. A coherent case could be put, for instance, for allowing the ownership of objects of considerable value, but not of land, even in small quantities. There is also an important ambiguity about the idea of the 'means of production'. According to Honoré the Soviet legal system incorporates the 'full liberal model' of ownership, but restricts the range of things which can be owned. The general principle of this restriction is that ownership of the means of production allows the development of inequality and exploitation. But it is difficult to distinguish the 'means of production' from other things; cars and houses (which can be owned in the Soviet Union) can be highly productive in any reasonable sense of that word. In any case, a system which allowed for the ownership of cars and houses, but did not allow a builder to own enough capital equipment to employ other men, would fit on to the continuum only imperfectly. Nevertheless, we can generally arrange answers to the question of the application of the full liberal model of ownership, or what can be owned, along a line.

Crossing this continuum are an infinite number of other lines along which can be measured the extent of the rights that owners have. It is an infinite number because each individual who wanted to have a 'position' on ownership could prescribe precisely a bundle of rights which he thought were proper for each good or class of goods, and the number of possible goods or classifications of goods has no limit. On these lines 'milestone' questions concern whether people can pass on their goods as legacies, whether they can destroy them and how much of the income they can retain. There is no equivalent of value on which to organise these lines; they have to be vaguely envisaged as measuring the completeness of the bundle of rights which men can exercise over objects.

The infinite number of lines can be simplified to one, which still allows the great majority of positions people actually hold (as opposed to those which they might conceivably hold) to be shown. This line measures the completeness of rights which can be exercised over the means of production, broadly defined. Thus we can produce a two-dimensional map (see figure 1) of moral views of ownership:

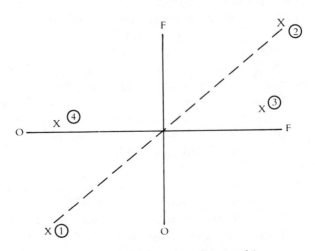

Figure 1 Moral views of ownership

The horizontal axis represents the range of things which can be owned from the minimum normally conceived (O) to the maximum conceivable (F). The vertical axis represents the completeness of owners' rights, also from minimal (O) to maximum conceivable (F). The dotted diagonal line represents a range of positions on ownership which can be seen as a political 'spectrum' from 'left' (1) to 'right' (2). Although roughly recognisable, this spectrum is not to be taken too seriously; it represents vagueness multiplied by vagueness, an abstract of an abstract.

I have identified four positions on this map.

1 An anarchist position of a minimal range of things which can be owned and minimal rights over them, though these rights are forfeited (by comparison with other societies) to the 'community' rather than the 'state'.

2 An 'old liberal' or 'American conservative' position which
  endorses a very complete and well-protected set of rights
  constituting ownership which can be of a very wide variety
  of things.
3 My own position, one variant of English conservatism,
  approving a comparatively large sphere of private ownership, but transferring some rights of owners to the state as
  compared with the old liberal position.
4 The position expressed by the Soviet legal system in which
  both rights and range are limited, but the restriction of range
  is much greater than that of rights as compared with the old
  liberal position.

THE CONSERVATIVE CASE FOR OWNERSHIP

Conservatism is normally associated with a belief in private ownership, so much so that a conservative, like myself, who has reserva-
tions both about the extent of owners' rights *vis-à-vis* the state and
(to a lesser extent) about whether some kinds of things ought to be
privately owned ought to justify himself under the semantic
equivalent of the Trade Descriptions Act. As I have stressed, it is
difficult to argue the pros and cons of ownership without qualifying
three aspects: what can be owned, what is the extent of ownership,
and what is the nature of the entity in which ownership is vested?

For instance, consider a large manufacturing company which has
several plants and many thousands of employees. It might be
owned by the state; it might be a public company owned by a large
variety of individuals and institutions and run by professional
managers; or it might be a private company owned by a single
family, the descendants of its founder. Some of the advantages of
non-private ownership, such as the ability to employ at every level
on merit or the capacity to expand to the most efficient level, might
accrue both to the state corporation and to the public company, but
not to the private company. Some of the advantage of private
ownership, particularly the constant need for the organisation to be
aware of its fiscal self-determination and thus to exercise a proper
self-control, might accrue to both kinds of non-state company.
(They might accrue to the state corporation, but there are theoretical

reasons, backed by empirical evidence, for considering this possibility to be less likely.) But some of the advantages of private ownership, such as the assumption that the firm is an end in itself rather than an instrument for furthering careers and providing salaries and that its time-horizons are unlimited, only accrue to the private company, not the public one.

To some extent the case for ownership must depend on the nature of the entity which owns, and also on the object owned. All over the world the state plays a dominant part in forestry; the time horizons of private land-owners and their financial constraints severely inhibit their capacity to grow trees. To cite an extreme example: it takes 60 years for a sweet chestnut tree to grow to full maturity and productivity. A family farm, run with dynastic foresight, might plant sweet chestnut trees, and the state might. It is less easy to imagine a public company doing so, but it might, because there is not only the question of the income return, but also of the enhancement of capital value.

Finally, if ownership is limited in certain ways it may simply not matter whether it is 'public' or 'private'. The question of the BBC's status seems to be merely technical in respect of freedom of speech and the same can be argued about the National Trust. The Trust is a private organisation which owns some of the most beautiful land and buildings in England, but it is bound by the terms of its charter to preserve and maintain those properties and is further constrained by the supervision of the Charity Commissioners through its receipt (in effect) of public money. To someone who wants the Trust to achieve the maximum conceivable success in its aims it may be a fine and trivial question as to whether it should be a public or a private body. What does matter is that it should be honest, efficient and true to its aims; the quality of its personnel and the moral ambience in which they move are far more important in determining these matters than is any formal distinction of 'public' and 'private'.

TWO CONSERVATIVE POSITIONS

Despite all these qualifications it is possible to consider the case for private ownership in general. There are two kinds of conservative case for ownership, based on entirely different philosophical assumptions.

The first kind can be called 'absolutist' and is based on the concept of rights. It asserts that ownership is the consequence of human rights which are above and beyond the state. As a consequence of these rights people come to own things which they have properly claimed and, to some extent, created by their labours. The existence of the state cannot be justified if it seeks to confiscate what is legitimately owned; if it does, it attacks the fundamental rights of individuals and therefore forfeits its right to demand their allegiance. Stealing is wrong irrespective of what positive laws say and whether it is persons or states who do it. This is the old liberal view, famously expressed in John Locke's *Two Treatises of Government* and recently in Robert Nozick's *Anarchy, State and Utopia*. It leaves certain questions unanswered, especially the question of the cumulative effects of inherited wealth and how it can be applied as a doctrine relevant to, and claiming the allegiance of, people born in social circumstances which offer them little or nothing to which they can lay claim or with which they can mix their labour. Scorn has been poured on this political theory by many of the most prestigious of modern theorists, including John Plamenatz, Brian Barry and Roger Scruton, and I have no wish to add to it. My rejection of the theory can be expressed as rejection of its first premise, that human beings can be said to have rights outside the context of a regulated society.

The substantive conclusion of this argument can be reached from another direction. This is a version of the 'slippery slope' argument, absolutist without being fundamentalist. This says that ownership must be absolutely protected, because the slightest weakening of the institution tends to cause its collapse; thus all forms of bad ownership have to be accepted because to reject them is to destroy the system of ownership and all the advantages which go with it. It is undeniably true that to believe in private ownership one must accept *some* forms and examples of ownership which have overwhelmingly bad consequences, but to have to accept *all* and reject all forms of state control would seem to be one of those prescriptions which insists on throwing the baby out with the bath water. The argument is remarkably parallel to that put by theorists in the Soviet Union who oppose all forms of decentralisation and profit-seeking factory autonomy. This argument is not theoretical, it is a matter of practice and judgement. The extent to which the state can interfere with private ownership while retaining its advantages can only be learnt by experience. And the experience of state ownership in Britain, especially of development control based on the nationalisation of development rights, suggests that many important advantages can be accrued by the state and the public without weakening the incentives of owners. Von Hayek called this 'the new feudalism', but a conservative is entitled to say that his objections were both fundamentalist and liberal and thus not truly conservative.

Most conservatives defend the institution of private ownership on balance, in practice and in terms of a variety of social values, rather than absolutely. There are powerful arguments for and against full ownership of a wide variety of things. Those who oppose it can say that it is inegalitarian and that it concentrates power away from democratic and popular controls. According to one version of justice, hereditary ownership is a fundamental injustice. It is also said to have a corrupting effect on people's sense of duty and community. All these arguments can be countered by those who favour ownership. A full system of ownership allows people to plan their lives more completely, to accumulate and live without work; it is thus much more compatible with personal autonomy and self-determination. Ownership protects people from the state; in systems which limit accumulation everybody is dependent on the state and conformity is easy to ensure. Thus it is not only those who are able to accumulate who benefit from accumulation: the whole quality of life is enhanced. The possibility of being rich may excite envy, but also allows hope. One sense of justice suggests powerfully that those who create wealth should be allowed to accumulate and store it and not have it confiscated to spread among the officials of the state and those defined as having 'needs'.

These arguments are complex and irresoluble; they involve conflicting values and conflicting interpretations of what seems to be the same value, as well as rival interpretations of how life is and speculations about how it might be. But there is one form of argument for private ownership which has recurred for many hundreds of years which seems less speculative and less easy to oppose by an equal and opposite argument. This is the argument from good husbandry.

The argument applies primarily to land, but by extension it is relevant to other kinds of fixed capital. It is a form of the incentives argument because its core is the claim that land is best looked after by people who have the most to gain from looking after it well. Only if a person receives the income from land, can use it and manage it, only if he has security and unlimited time in the possession of it and can transfer it in any way he chooses, is he likely to equate his own interests with the general productive capacity of the land he works. In short, only if he more or less owns it will he manure it and hedge it and ditch it and avoid over-cropping it. To suggest a link between ownership and good husbandry does not, of course, imply that all private owners are good farmers; it is obvious that in reality some of them are both incompetent and short-sighted. It supports only the judgement that aggregatively, usually private ownership of land is better for the value of that land than is any alternative arrangement.

The argument from good husbandry is supported by a more detailed argument which can be expressed as a formal model or as a historical experience; this argument has been called 'the tragedy of the commons'. Consider a system of grazing common land, once normal in England. As the number of beasts in a given area of land increases there must come a point at which an additional beast will mean that the common is over-grazed: its rate of grazing is faster than its rate of growth, it is denuded, suffers ecological catastrophe; the beasts die and the common is rendered worthless. The grazier responsible – in the terms of modern theory he can be called the catastrophic marginal grazier – has no disincentive to avoid the catastrophe. He is better off by inducing it, because at least he gets some grazing before the collapse occurs, whereas if he were to be 'public spirited' someone else would play the role of the catastrophic marginal. (This is assuming that graziers are ecologically informed; of course, the same consequences occur if they are not.) With privately held land this would not happen; owners have every incentive to maintain and enhance its quality and every disincentive to induce ecological collapse.

The tragedy of the commons suggests a generally applicable argument that private ownership (or something very much like it) is better for the productive capacity of a society's assets. This form of argument does rely on judgements about 'human nature' and is only valid where we can assume that a substantial number of actors are predominantly self-interested. (How big the number is would depend on many things. In some cases it might only be one actor; it would rarely need to be as many as half the total.) As I have already suggested, such judgements are, ultimately, only speculative and the evidence only circumstantial. But it does seem quite powerful; private agriculture is generally much more effective than any alternative. Communal and state agriculture appears to work less well except for a short time, over which communal spirit can be dominant, or where the number of people cooperating is sufficiently small and their collective rights sufficiently great that they can think like owners.

Introspectively, thinking like an owner is quite different from thinking like a non-owner. I once lived in a house which was owned by a university; I paid nothing to maintain it and gained nothing from any increase in its value. In all honesty, I was less than vigilant about the kind of damage which cumulatively can lead to decay. I once laughed when water came through the ceiling. Now I am a freeholder; if the cost of any deterioration in my house is allowed to grow beyond the unavoidable minimum, I have to pay. I stand to gain from any enhancement in its value, so I look after it a great deal better. I may be enormously selfish, but the evidence suggests that the spirit of cooperation and communal action, though it exists, is as limited in most people as it is in me.

The good husbandry argument and the model of the tragedy of the commons generate a utilitarian defence of ownership of considerable speculative power, though not of demonstrable validity. But arguments of similar power can be generated in the opposite direction. Take, for instance, the 'tragedy of the trams'. At time t Gotham City has an extensive system of trams. These are publicly owned and most citizens do most of their travelling on them. On most routes there is a tram every ten minutes; on average the citizens pay 15 dinars per journey and the average journey to work takes 20 minutes. The trams make a profit. Then, at time $t + 1$, some citizens buy motor cars. They are able to get to work for ten dinars and their average time is ten minutes for the same range of journeys. So far it makes little difference to the trams. At time $t + 2$, the cars have started to affect the trams and each other. It now takes 20 minutes to get to work by car, 25 by tram. The cost has gone up to 15 dinars by car and (to cover falling revenue and because it takes longer) to 20 dinars by tram.

Finally, at time $t + 5$ the cars have clogged up the roads. The average length of a journey is now 40 minutes, however you go, and it costs 30 dinars by car, 35 by tram. Gotham City is much more polluted and people complain constantly about the traffic jams and the infrequency of tram services and the huge taxes they have to pay to cover the deficit on the trams and to pay for road improvements.

Alternatively, take the tragedy of the mountains. Flatsville is in a valley, surrounded by attractive green mountains. These are virtually uninhabited because of the relatively high cost of building on them. The overwhelming majority of people do not want the mountains to be built on; they are beautiful to look at, easy and interesting to visit and they contribute to the cleanness of the atmosphere over the city. But Flatsville is in the United States of America and it is very difficult for any public body to prevent private land being developed because of the Fifth Amendment of the Constitution (or, arguably, the way in which judges interpret the Fifth Amendment). There are people who want to live on the mountains and money to be made for owners and developers. These owners and developers are in the same position as the catastrophic marginal grazier on the common: however public-spirited they are, there is really nothing they can do to stop the development, so they might as well make some money.

The tragedy of the commons suggests that in some instances, based on utilitarian values, there are powerful arguments for private ownership. But the tragedy of the trams suggests that there are examples which pose an equally strong case for public ownership and the restriction of private ownership. After all, private agriculture has produced its own ecological catastrophes like the dust bowls of pre-war Oklahoma. And the tragedy of the mountains suggests a case for the restriction of the concept of ownership by English-style development control.

It is conservative to insist on the importance and relevance of the case for private ownership. But it is also conservative (as opposed to liberal, socialist, or communist) to avoid dogmatic and over-arching theories and to see, also, the other cases. Conservatism is uniquely subtle and flexible in this respect; it acknowledges that the question of which of these models is relevant to a particular policy, and to what degree, is one of judgement, the very stuff of good politics.

9

FREEDOM

I take it that 'freedom' and 'liberty' are two labels for the same concept. However it is named, it is one of the most difficult concepts in political philosophy and has an unparalleled capacity to generate confusion and paradox. We can enslave children in formal education and yet free them from their ignorance. According to one broad and persistent European mode of argument, true freedom can be found only in the pursuit of a high and metaphysical goal such as duty or God or natural law: the sensual pursuit of pleasure is the opposite of freedom, an enslavement to passion; 'liberty' must not be confused with 'licence'. But there is an opposite tradition, that of Hume and Bentham (and W. S. Gilbert, for that matter), which sees law and duty as the most common constraints preventing the individual from doing what he wants. Men can be freed from their enslavement to drugs or left free to enjoy them. They can be colonised to free them from primitive and ignorant tyrannies and they can be liberated from their colonisers. Freedom is a concept of plausible opposites. Rousseau's call that people should be 'forced to be free' is almost, but not quite, logically unacceptable.

One modern attempt to reconcile these paradoxes and contradictions which has had considerable influence is Sir Isaiah Berlin's distinction between 'two concepts' of liberty. Berlin suggests that there is a clear difference between those who propose liberty in the 'negative' sense and those who propose it in the 'positive' sense. Negative freedom is 'freedom from'; it is the absence of constraints upon individual choice and an increase in freedom can only take place by the removal of some constraint or constraints. Positive liberty, on the other hand, is 'freedom to', the progress of the soul toward a higher state, a state of liberation.

In the history of ideas, these two concepts of liberty have very different characteristics. Negative liberty represents a relatively clear and uniform position and one which is predominantly 'Anglo-Saxon' (in De Gaulle's sense). It has been a concept developed by liberal utilitarians; Jeremy Bentham is perhaps its most uncompromising exponent and it has been developed in economic and legal theories as well as in social and political philosophy. It takes freedom to be the absence of coercive restraints upon individuals to pursue their wants, whatever those wants happen to be. The positive concept, by contrast, is central to the theories and prescriptions of a bewilderingly wide variety of writers, mainly from outside the English-speaking countries, who believe that the significant sense in which they propose that men should be freed or liberated relates to some 'higher', 'finer' or 'deeper' side to their natures, and not *necessarily* to their existing wants. The category thus includes, among others, Kantians, Hegelians and Marxists as well as many nationalist and religious writers.

There is no doubt which side Berlin is on. The positive concept is logically so all-embracing that support for it seems to melt into the position that freedom can never be bad and that whatever is good can be called freedom. By allowing so many forms of compulsion to be called true freedom, positive liberty provides just so many moral licences for tyranny and intolerance. Support for the negative concept rather than the positive suggests support for capitalism and competitive elections, so much so that Berlin has been accused of being a cold war propagandist. This is an odd allegation, not least because it would be very odd if a political philosopher who was putting forward substantive views on liberty did not, thereby, favour one social system over another. But there is no doubt, in several senses, which side he is on.

My quarrel with Berlin is much more formal. As far as I am concerned his account of the two traditions is profound and informative. If positive and negative could be clearly distinguished and if we have to choose (two very big 'ifs', as will become apparent), then I would be on his side. But, at the formal level, there are *not* two concepts of liberty. Depending on what one means by 'concept', either there is one concept or there are an indefinitely large number. This is a complex argument, but it is relatively simple to establish that there can be no such thing as a purely or even primarily negative or positive approach to freedom.

Negative libertarians have, just as much as their opponents, a positive conception of what man is. It is a very different conception, because it conceives men as bundles of wants without concerning itself with the origins or the quality of those wants. However, it would be absurd to claim that nothing exists in the human mind except self-conscious wants. The suicide has an instinct of self-preservation, the philistine has creative capacities, the monk has a sexual impulse: these things exist even if, in each case, the person chooses to override them. It will not do to say that the negative libertarians offer freedom to man himself whereas their opponents seek to liberate only an abstract and idealised concept of man. Both draw selectively on aspects of the mind which can be said to exist.

Conversely, all positive theorists can be construed as making statements about constraints upon the aspects of man they seek to liberate. To Marxists, capitalist socio-economic relations and the alienation which stems from them are an obstacle to human development. To Christians, corruption and lack of faith are constraints upon the soul's potential for salvation. To cultural nationalists, particularly in small nations, the international mass-media are an obstacle to the preservation and expression of people's identity. Every positive theorist is also arguing 'freedom from' in some sense and every negative one 'freedom to'.

A far more accurate description of the formal structure of the concept of freedom is given by Gerald MacCallum in his essay 'Negative and Positive Freedom'. MacCallum insists that 'freedom is thus always *of* something (an agent or agents), *from* something, *to* do, not do, become or not become something; it is a triadic relation.' This apparently simple formula admits of a wealth of complexity. This complexity carries an enormous capacity to compare people, and much of this capacity lies in the logical relation between the 'agent' and the constraints on his freedom and the difficulty of distinguishing between them.

CONSTRAINTS ON FREEDOM

The only constraints which limit freedom are the consequences of human agency. Rousseau said that: 'The nature of things does not madden us, only ill-will does.' Peter Strawson has suggested that it is only rational to talk about unfreedom where it is appropriate to be resentful. In other words, it is both unconventional and futile to talk about one's freedom being restricted if nobody is doing the restricting in any sense.

In Rousseau's rather dramatic terms there are some things which might impede our actions which are not relevant to liberty because they are part of the nature of things. The laws of physics (or, rather, the existence of physical laws) fall more clearly into this category than does anything else. The question does not arise as to whether I am free or unfree to flap my arms and fly out of the earth's atmosphere; the thing is impossible. There is some doubt, necessarily, about what is the content of this kind of impossibility, but no doubt that it has a very large content. Another part of the impossible category is that which lies outside my own personal capacities. I (meaning the author, not 'one') cannot paint in the Cubist style. In any normal or rational sense of freedom I am quite free to paint in the Cubist style, for I live in England, not in Albania. But I am intuitively satisfied that I have an innate incapacity to do so. Having allowed incapacity in principle as irrelevant to freedom it does become very difficult to distinguish incapacities from unfreedoms. To take a very crude example, I may be incapable of practising my trade as a carpenter because I have no hands. But what if the state has cut off my hands? Certainly it would be very odd to say that if the state passed an injunction prohibiting me from practising as a carpenter it would be restricting my freedom, but if it cut off my hands, it wouldn't. It would even be difficult to refute the claim that my inability to paint in the Cubist style (or any other style, for that matter) is the consequence of some inhibiting system of socialisation whereby my liberty and my human potential has been constrained.

The final category of impossibilities is also easier to establish in principle than it is to describe in detail. Some social arrangements are unavoidable: buses and trains can only run at particular times, television and radio programmes cannot all be broadcast at once, school lessons and university lectures must be organised according to some ordered scheme or other. There must be at least some cases of unavoidable arrangements which are not relevant to freedom. But if the bus timetable is organised to prevent working-class people from visiting the countryside, or to make it difficult for poor people to watch horse-races, then that is relevant to freedom. And the restriction need not be deliberate or conspiratorial: callousness or the tacit assumption of certain social priorities must also be treated as 'ill will'.

Thus, if anything can properly be said to be impossible, the question of freedom does not arise. True, Albert Camus in *L'Homme Révolté* discusses a range of writers in a state of 'metaphysical' rebellion, protesting at the very nature of things. But what might be said to be the conceivable purpose of such protest and to whom is it addressed? It could only be addressed to God and, since his non-existence is a necessary condition of the 'absurdity' of the universe, they are left protesting to God about his failure to exist.

If one is unfree to do anything it must be possible to do it, at least remotely. And, indeed, this is clearly the case with most of the things which we normally talk about as constraints on our liberty. Rules are made to be broken, laws even more so. Bullies are there to be stood up to. Contracts and conventions can be flouted. All these actions carry a cost or the risk of a cost, but none is impossible. This is a paradoxical consequence, but it is a paradox which must be accepted because it is an essential part of the concept of freedom. Thus there is a sense in which everything which stops a person doing anything is within himself. The law makes us unfree to import cocaine, but only our state of mind can actually prevent us from doing it. We might fear being caught or respect the law as such or consider the importation of cocaine immoral quite independently of the law. Whichever it is, the constraint is ultimately within us, because it is possible to have absolute confidence in one's ability to get away with it, or be indifferent to punishment and so on.

Even so, we normally talk about the law and its coercive machinery as if *it* were the constraint and not our fear of it or respect for it. Both ways of talking can be consistent and coherent: every constraint on our freedom lies both inside us and outside us. Which version we choose depends on making a moral judgement about the circumstances in which people ought to be regarded as free. For instance, were officials of the Third Reich free to dissociate themselves from its anti-semitic activities?

The range of things which might count as constraints on liberty can be divided into three categories which have morally significant differences between them. First, there is the *coercive enforcement* of rules, especially the laws enforced by the state. These are assumed to be relevant to liberty in all normal and conventional uses of the word. Second, there are *institutions*, many forms of social organisation which impose costs upon choice. Two of these stand out as of greater importance than all others. One is the institution of money and its consequences, including the difficulty of making it if you indulge in many levels of non-conformist behaviour (keeping your own time, for instance, or saying what you think). Then there is ostracism, for money does not matter if nobody will have social or economic relations with you, a deprivation Captain Boycott experienced in its extreme form. Third, there are *inhibitions*, the restriction of the personality through socialisation so that people are prevented from doing things, even though no costs are imposed upon them. Anything which can be called 'programming', 'brain-washing' or 'conditioning' falls into this category: conscience, timidity, self-deprecation, a self-limiting perception of one's role in society can all limit people's action. This is therefore the biggest category of constraint on action, the most important and the most dubious. But it cannot be dismissed on the grounds that it alone is internal to the agent. All constraints on action are, in an ultimate sense, internal. The law only constrains us if we are frightened or respectful of it or lack the ability to deceive its agents. Being sacked only matters if you care.

Consider two famous examples in the light of this trichotomy. There is the famous question of whether the penniless tramp is free to have tea in the Dorchester Hotel. No coercive rule prevents him as it would prevent a black man outside a prestigious hotel in Johannesburg. In that sense he is free to do it; all he has to do is get together certain resources and be prepared to spend them. In that sense he is as free to have tea in the hotel as the wealthy businessman who has no time to take tea properly and rather freer than the duke who has been forbidden tea and carbohydrates by his doctor. But the tramp might well argue that this is a trivial sense of freedom and that the economic institutions of society conspire to prevent him having any money or a valid credit card, so that it would be nonsense to say that he was 'effectively', 'really' or 'truly' free to take tea in the Dorchester. Even if he could scrape together enough money, he might add, he has much greater needs to spend it on and the real cost of tea in the Dorchester would always be too high in his case. Finally, it might never occur to him to have tea in the Dorchester. Downtrodden all his life, he would assume that such a place was 'not for the likes of him', or he might fear the contemptuous treatment a man of his demeanour would receive from the hotel staff. It could be argued that a society in which all were free to eat in the place of their choice could only exist if the social system no longer created inhibitions in people like the tramp. Such a society would be 'classless'.

Or take the idea of the 'permissive society', with specific reference to the question of whether people are free to have homosexual intercourse. Of course, there are many societies in which this is prohibited by law, though such laws are very difficult to enforce by their very nature. More effective constraints might lie in the attitudes of employers and local society to people who show signs of homosexual soliciting or live with members of their own sex. Finally, there might be societies in which, perhaps for religious reasons, homosexuality was considered so dreadful and distasteful that it would be almost impossible to conceive an active desire for it even though there were no laws against it and no institutional procedures for making life difficult for homosexuals.

One thing is, I hope, established: there are no clear and indisputable distinctions between what is relevant to freedom and what is not. John Stuart Mill offered 'one very simple principle' of liberty: 'the only purpose for which power can be rightfully exercised over any member of a civilised community, against his will, is to prevent harm to others. His own good, either physical or moral, is not a sufficient warrant.' This is anything but 'one very simple principle'. The forms of power which inhibit liberty are so diverse that it can be translated into a myriad of different principles. Mill himself was keen that people should be drawn away from vulgar and corrupt pleasures and towards the higher and finer aspects of the culture. To this end he was prepared to sanction that they be influenced, propagandised, lectured and ostracised, commercially if necessary. The state had its part to play in these influences. The distinction between what he proposed in his arguments about culture and morality and what he opposed in his 'one very simple principle' is not the clear and morally significant distinction he thought it was.

AGENTS: WHEN IS A PERSON NOT HIMSELF?

Many things which can count as constraints on liberty can equally well be treated as part of the agent himself. A central theme in

Western liberalism has been religious toleration, the freedom to practise one's own religion. The assumption of this argument is that the religion, once chosen, is a part of oneself; impediments to its expression and practice are constraints on freedom. But this can be inverted, so that a religion is an imposition upon a person; its levels of faith restricting thought and its moral values inhibiting conduct. This is the normal way in which some religions are discussed. The Moonies are said to enslave, indoctrinate or brainwash their followers; their religion is portrayed much more often as a threat to freedom than as an expression of it. But the same language could be applied equally coherently to much more respectable religions such as Islam and Roman Catholicism. The doctrine of either can be highly restrictive of sexual and intellectual freedom. The effectiveness of religious propaganda and education, highlighted by the Jesuit claim that a child, once educated, can be made a Catholic forever, is something with which no secular state can compete. Nor can a system of positive law compete with the cosmic and eternal deprivations which serve as sanctions in either Islam or Catholicism.

A parallel argument concerns taste. Liberal economists and public administrators invariably assume, and often assert dogmatically, that taste is the final and innermost sanctum of individual freedom. A person's choice of what to consume, whether in food and drink or in music and books, is the thing most unambiguously part of himself; no government should presume to legislate about taste. But it is inaccurate to portray tastes as something which are innate to the individual. They are formed and developed and influenced from the outside, by families and educators and advertisers. Their development can be among the most severe and tragic inhibitions of a person's life and range of options, even when they constitute the minimal conceivable interference with anyone else. This is particularly true of addictive commodities, certainly when the addition is physical, but almost as clearly when it is psychological. People's lives can be destroyed by heroin and alcohol, even by tobacco; they can be pretty well ruined by carbohydrates. To say of somebody whose life has been transformed by addiction that he is free because the law did not prevent him from becoming addicted is, to borrow an expression used by Berlin in a similar context, to mock his condition. John Stuart Mill's insistence on the non-interference of the law with the right to take drugs seems fanatical to the point of cruelty. Even tastes cannot be treated as a certain and undeniable part of the person himself about which no legislation is proper; there is some force in the old idea of slavery to the passions.

Many of the differences between the wide variety of views of freedom can be envisaged as points on a continuum arranged as a set of different conceptions of what constitutes a person and what are the constraining influences upon that person's freedom. At one extreme of that continuum is the view of man held by Bentham and the classical economists. Bentham declared himself unconcerned with men as they ought to be or might have become or could be in the future; his subject was man as he exists, unmodified. Anything which restrains a mild desire, whatever it is, limits his freedom and cannot enhance it. I cannot be liberated from addiction if I want to take the drug, nor can education free me from ignorance if ignorance is what I want.

At the other end of the continuum are a set of approaches to the identity of the agent which Berlin calls 'the retreat to the inner citadel'. These take no account at all of the desires which a person may happen to have. Instead they start with an essence of man which, through a variety of circumstances, he may have lost sight of completely. He is a religious being, so the search for God is his only liberation. He is 'human', so communism is his only true freedom. He is sexual, so liberty consists in the eradication of complexes. He is creative, so education must liberate him. He is Irish, so a republic is necessary and sufficient for his freedom.

One of these extremes is exemplified by a single approach, the other by an indefinitely wide variety. Both have had a powerful appeal, but both have obvious flaws. Those approaches which 'retreat to the inner citadel' clearly attract the criticism that they are both nonsense and dangerous. There are no limits to what might be claimed as the content of the inner citadel and, morally, such concepts of the human essence can be said to license, and have been used to justify, every possible tyranny over man in the name of man's true freedom. But the other extreme can be subjected to parallel criticisms. Conceptually, it limits the ways in which we can talk about freedom to a narrow and simple range: liberation from want, ignorance or addiction cannot be included. Morally, this approach invites the charge of callousness because whatever happens to the agent is seen as his own responsibility.

Ideas of the person and of freedom which lie between these two extremes must all take their concepts of the agent partly, but not entirely, from the existing reality; rather than being either essential or empirical they must be hypothetical. That is, they must take men as they are but assume them to be in more favourable circumstances. Thus they argue that freedom for the most part is not mere absence of external restraint, but absence of restraint for man in the condition of being non-addicted, sane, rational, fully informed, having his basic needs provided or some other minimal set of circumstances in which his choices could be said to be his own.

Hypothetical conceptions of the agent can take many forms, but they can be divided broadly into two main kinds. First, there are those in which the set of conditions requires only that the individual agent is of a certain form or reaches a certain standard. Providing he is adult, sane and sober and not infatuated, addicted or indoctrinated, and reasonably well informed, then his decisions are his own and only immediately external factors can be said to restrict his freedom. These are hypothetical – individual concepts of freedom.

A second class of hypothetical argument about freedom insists that the agent can only be treated as himself insofar as he can be hypothesised under changed social conditions. In these arguments, existing social conditions are said to inhibit man and distort his perceptions. His interests can be inferred from his consciousness, but only by hypothesising him into a set of social conditions which do not distort his perceptions. There are some similarities between these hypothetical-social treatments of liberty and essential treatments, and Marxism (among other 'isms') has expressed arguments about freedom in both terms. But the differences are more important: essentialist conceptions of the agent include certain motives or objectives as necessary parts of the agent while hypothetical-social analyses state only the conditions under which we would know that motives or objectives were 'genuine'.

THE POSSIBLE CONCEPTS OF LIBERTY

Just as there are a range of concepts of agent and, in a corresponding and complementary way, a range of concepts of constraints on freedom, so there is also a considerable variety of what might be included as possible objectives in respect of which freedom can be constrained. Much of this follows from the relationships between the ideas of agent and constraint, but a narrowing of legitimate objectives is a feature of many ideas of freedom as, for example, when people distinguish between liberty and licence so that the generalised frustration of men's desire to consort with prostitutes is not relevant to freedom. A hierarchy of stipulations about objectives can be made. For example, a minimum requirement would be that they should be coherent. Some arguments imply that relevant objectives must be sustainable, not self-destructive as is the consumption of some drugs. A more rigorous requirement is that they should be aggregatable, capable of being spread throughout society. Some, at least, of personal economic objectives can only be achieved at the expense of closing the possibility of others achieving them. Stipulation can also be made that the objective be considered in an 'educated' way, the agent conceiving it attaining a certain level of rationality or information. And the concomitant of an 'essential' conception of the agent is that only objectives which are natural, derived from man's true nature, should be included.

Thus, in one sense there is one concept of freedom: all statements about freedom conform to a certain form. In another sense there is a wide range of concepts of freedom. This range can be summarised by a table which shows the different criteria applicable to the three parts of the triadic relation.

Agents	Constraints	Objectives
1 Immediate	1 Positive laws	1 Any
2 Hypothetical-individual	2 Social institutions	2 Any coherent
3 Hypothetical-social	3 Inhibitions	3 Coherent and sustainable
4 Essential		4 Sustainable and aggregatable
		5 Educated
		6 Natural

THE PRIMARY SENSE OF FREEDOM

There are many different ways of talking about freedom. One ideology's freedom is another's tyranny. There is a temptation to leave it at that, as an expression of intellectual pluralism, but if one were to leave the map in that state, so to speak, one would leave out an important aspect of the logical geography of the concept. Some of these ways of talking about liberty are highly marginal; they stretch the formal properties of the concept to a dubious limit. Conversely, one has a claim to be the primary sense. I refer to that implicit in capitalist law and economics: the freedom of a man, as he is, given only a fair access to significant information and a balanced mind, from the sovereign acts of the state, to conduct his life as he chooses. There are several arguments that suggest a special status for this sense of liberty which can be drawn from the criteria of formal conceptual correctness.

In the first place, the distinction of liberty in this sense is relatively precise and is normally dependent on legal and institutional judgements rather than on more transcendental theories of man and society. It is also close to a 'normal' and 'intuitive' sense in which we use the terms. We do feel entitled to say to a man who complains about the constraints imposed upon him by his marriage, his job, or his landlord, 'Well, you are free to leave', even if it is going to be difficult. If the same man complained about the state, it would not be reasonable to say, 'You're free to leave', even if it was in John Locke's day. In public political argument we often automatically assume the primacy of this sense of freedom. For instance, the National Council for Civil Liberties is *primarily* concerned with the relationship between individuals and the state as they are affected by the enforcement of laws. 'Free' collective bargaining, if it means anything, means a minimal legal interference by the state in the rights of firms and trade unions to conduct negotiations. Moreover, many of the institutional constraints that do not immediately fall into this definition collapse into, or are dependent on, the coercive legal power of the state.

This 'primary' sense of liberty is both clearer and closer to more established conventions than other ways of talking. It is also more useful: for the purpose of many of the most important arguments, whatever side we might wish to take and avoiding a degeneration into mere semantic competition, the focus on the relationship between the individual and the state allows us clear argument. The advantages of this sense of freedom are formal, not morally substantive. These advantages constitute good reasons for talking about freedom in this way; they are not reasons for action of any kind. Freedom is sometimes a bad thing. Many moralists consciously or unconsciously talk of freedom as if it is an overriding moral value:

whatever maximises freedom is necessarily right. This is as true of 'negative' and right-wing thinkers as of those who are essentialist and radical. Such talk equates 'freedom' with 'good' and leaves it a word of some emotive and rhetorical power, but useless in argument and analysis. One of the advantages of the primary sense of freedom is its clarity. Nothing which is clearly defined and recognisable can always be right.

It may seem inevitable, or at least ironically coincidental, that a conservative should stress the formal superiority of a concept of freedom which is very similar to the 'negative', 'capitalist' or 'Western' senses of freedom which are approved by many conservatives. But the coincidence is genuine; the kind of conservatism I am supporting does not regard such freedom of the individual from the state as being always a good thing. There can be many good reasons for the state coercing individuals which go well beyond the minimum requirements of social order. These can include the quality of the environment, the necessity of education and, at least to a limited extent, what Lord Devlin calls 'the moral fabric of society'. There are difficult judgements to be made in choosing between these, admittedly abstract and imprecise, goods, and the freedom of the individual in its primary sense. It must be wrong in at least some instances to favour freedom and I have pointed to some of these instances in other writings, particularly on the environment. Some are mentioned in other chapters of this book but a further group can be considered now, as part of the consideration of three particular applications of freedom.

Freedom of speech

Freedom of speech, as an application of the primary sense of the word, means an absence of interference by the state in acts of speech. But, having said that, there are a plethora of complex questions to answer: What counts as speech? Can we distinguish the state from other sources of constraints? How much freedom of speech is a good thing?

Outside of the pages of *1984* and other works of anti-Utopian fiction, states do not interfere with people's freedom to mutter to themselves while sitting on the toilet. It is very rare for states to punish people for things they may say in private conversations. Certainly people have been punished for such conversations; it happened under Hitler and under Stalin and it has happened in some 'developing' countries. But laws governing intimate conversations are rare: there is no substantial body of moral or political philosophy whether of 'left' or 'right' which justifies them and, in any case, they are bad laws because they can only be enforced selectively and arbitrarily. This is not to say that private talk is without its costs in any society; the expression of opinions, particularly unpopular ones, can always affect a person's social or economic standing.

It is also very difficult to distinguish speech from action. A person may say, 'There's been a terrible amount of violent crime round these parts.' This might be just a casual remark, but it might also be part of the collection procedure of a protection racket. At the stage at which criminals conspire and plan crimes they are only, after all, talking. Within disciplined organisations talk may be an order; the order may play a part in an act of murder. The right of picketing is, formally, the right of strikers to put their case to the workers who intend to replace them, but that is difficult to distinguish from threatening and obstructive behaviour. Demonstrations are an expression of political sentiment, but they, too, can be obstructive.

The cases of pickets and demonstrations do pose important questions about what the state should regulate, but they are of marginal importance to a consideration of freedom of speech. The classic arguments for freedom of expression – that debate is good for the intellect, that through it people learn to be tolerant and that it allows the truth to emerge – cannot plausibly be extended to massive and emotional congregations where no sentiment more complex than 'Scabs out' or 'Wogs out' can be expressed. It is not the speech which matters about pickets and demonstrations; it is the emotional fist which is made.

The issue of free speech does not seriously concern whether the state can allow a particular kind of statement to be made, but how, when and to whom it can be made. All legal systems regulate these aspects of expression and include laws against, for instance, libel, defacement by graffiti and threats. The English legal system has a vast battery of additional controls: the Official Secrets Act, 'D' notices withdrawing some articles on defence matters from newspapers and books, laws against blasphemous libel and obscene publications legislation. Some of these – the regulation of the content of books and plays, for example – have been eroded, but they have been replaced by others controlling the expression of opinion

128

through advertising, and the Race Relations Act. That the replace-
ments appear to exist to protect truth and virtue merely makes them
fashionable; it does not distinguish them from older forms of censorship which were also in line with the standards of their time.

Thus it is impossible to be 'against censorship' as a rigid principle
unless one is prepared to allow that youths can shout obscenities
menacingly at old ladies or that the powerful should be allowed
freely to spread slurs and lies about individuals or groups who
oppose them. Some public control of expression is necessary; the
important arguments are about what kind and on which forms of
expression.

In any case, it is very difficult to distinguish censorship from the
necessary consequences of the means of communication. All the
means of communication have controllers: magazine and newspaper
editors, television and radio producers, book publishers. These
controllers must make decisions about whom they allow to express
ideas. Such decisions must be based on criteria. The criteria of good
drama or news or poetry incorporate standards which cannot,
ultimately, be distinguished from moral and political standards. In
practice this may mean that, for instance, the BBC has a strong
tendency to select plays which have a certain kind of dramatic 'bite'
and which are 'serious'. These would be plays with a critical or
humanist perspective which tend to attack existing social mores and
institutions and thus to favour the 'left'. Even if this is not a correct
account of the bias, there must be some bias. Spokesmen for the
BBC freely admit to the exclusion of, among other things, obscenity, overt partisan expression, libel and racialism.

The BBC has a typically and uniquely English status. It is a
broadcasting corporation, funded from the public purse but not
controlled directly by the government and, to some extent, specifically excluded from such control. Nevertheless, it is ultimately
subject to the financial and regulatory powers of the government.
This curious status is not of merely contingent interest; it is on the
interpretation of this status that any judgement must be based as to
whether the existence of BBC editorial policy is in itself a form of
censorship and a constraint on the freedom of speech. The case that
it is censorship would seem to be much stronger if the corporation
had a legal monopoly – which it did from 1922 until 1953.

At this point the argument seems to have reduced itself to
dependence on a highly technical point: the exact status of the BBC.

But, from an author's point of view, the sense of freedom or censorship is always going to consist in what is allowed, not of the status of the agency doing the allowing. In the United States, where the public sector is only a tiny and specialised part of broadcasting, one might say to any author, from the point of view of the primary sense of freedom, 'You are free to sell your work and have it produced. You will, of course, have to find a company prepared to take it on. . . .' But this is of little compensation if there are certain kinds of work which no company will take on. And the range of forms and ideas on American television does seem to be rather narrower than that on the BBC, even considered in isolation. It does seem to make sense to talk of 'private censorship': the idea that one can start one's own television channel seems almost meaningless in view of the prevailing commercial and financial pressures. Yet, considered in terms of the primary sense of freedom, there is free expression on American television, as much as there is in, say, American publishing.

Thus, in terms of the primary sense of freedom, the issue of freedom of speech or expression seems to resolve itself into a criterion which is both pedantic and trivial, the question of whether the censors and controllers of the means of communication are public or private. The question of whether they are competitive or monopolistic ought, surely, to be much more important. In any case, in most societies the state licenses broadcasting and often other means of communication. But, though the primary sense may be only one way of talking about freedom of expression, it still seems to provide a clearer distinction than is otherwise available. In practice, it is inevitable that there should be people who control the important means of communication and that they should assume certain standards in exercising such control. The extreme case of 'free speech' would seem to be a set of arrangements in which anybody can communicate anything at any time to any audience he chooses. This is not conceivable in a society of any size or complexity. Attempting to reach this condition could only lead to the population being forced to listen to the dreary rantings of thousands of humanist poets who would quickly emerge once the constraints of supply and demand had been removed.

In view of these enormous complexities, only a fool could say that he was in favour of 'free speech' as such. The questions which do matter concern how the controllers of communication should be chosen, organised and themselves controlled and what, if anything, should be prohibited from all forms of communication by the state. The answers to both questions depend on the objectives one assumes. Plausible and widely shared objectives seem, in practice, to conflict. The highest possible level of intellectual and artistic quality is an end in itself, but those capable of producing it often seem to offend popular mores. The highest possible level of debate, whether scientific, philosophical or political, would be generally considered desirable, but extremely difficult to define.

Whatever the objectives, at least within this range, there is no easy formula determining arrangements which might provide them. 'Objectivity' is not possible: the choice of what to communicate cannot be made without moral standards and there exists no language to describe social affairs which does not itself carry evalua-tions to its listeners: it is the familiar question of 'terrorists' and 'freedom fighters'. It is a fairly clear principle to insist that people tell the truth, that what purport to be 'brute facts' involve no lies. But it is also fairly trivial: the selection and interpretation of facts and their incorporation into arguments all require evaluations. 'Objectivity' must not be confused with 'political balance', which is merely the prudent avoidance of overt offence to those who may become the communicators' masters, in one sense or another, in a two-party system.

Nor does 'democracy' provide a solution. The 'people' en masse lack the time, the will and the expertise to control the means of communication in anything larger than the most simple society. In practice, democratisation could only sanction yet another set of controllers and standards.

For what it is worth, the anomalous arrangements of post-war Britain seem to me to serve the important purposes of a system of communication with as great a variety of artistic expression and as broad a debate as exists or has existed anywhere else. These arrange-ments consist of a publicly financed corporation not directly subject to state control and a set of loosely regulated commercial rivals. Nevertheless it would be wrong to suggest that these provide some kind of formula or right answer; their relative success originates at least as much in the mores of the controllers as in the arrangements through which they control. The question of how the system can best be maintained and enhanced is one susceptible to subtle and particular judgements rather than to rigid formulae.

Nor can there be any right answer to the question of direct criminal legislation against forms of expression. Some forms of expression, in some contexts, can be offensive or dangerous: the kind of pictures which appear in *Penthouse* ought not to be allowed to appear on a wall poster between a first school and an old people's home. It is the size and definition of the set of prohibited expressions which is a matter of serious debate, not its existence. What does seem to be an irrefutable part of the traditional liberal case is that there should be no absolute ban on the expression of ideas, however unconventional. There are no standards on which to base such a ban and the level of debate could only suffer as a result of it. People should be able to say that the state is unnecessary and wicked and should be destroyed by violence or that black people are genetically inferior and one should be allowed to buy and sell them or that the earth is about to be destroyed by divine retribution. But the context in which they are allowed to say these things should be controlled: as a rule of thumb about the currently available means of communication, I would suggest that we need no limits on books or magazines, but that it is right (as well as unavoidable) that there are strict controls on what is shown on 'prime time' television.

Self-determination: the freedom of peoples

'Liberation' movements and fronts; the Free Wales Army; 'set my people free': we often talk of freedom referring not to individuals, but to collectivities, nations and tribes. It is a way of talking with a lineage that goes back to ancient Greece, and the principle of self-determination has been an accepted principle of international relations since 1918. The relationship between this sense of freedom and all other senses raises a difficult question. 'Self-determination' is a misleading expression; tribes and nations do not have 'selves' in any ordinary sense. Who is freed when a nation is liberated, and from what?

Whatever the relation of ideas of collective freedom to those of individual freedom, the principle of self-determination faces several major conceptual difficulties. First, it is possible to have more than one kind of identity, to be Ukrainian and Soviet, Scottish and British, Ulster and Irish and British, or Texan and American and Jewish. Africa, Arabia and South America are known to have tribes, but Europe has, too: it consists not only of Frenchmen and

Germans, but also of Bretons and Basques, Ladins and Lapps. One modern piece of research, by Erik Allardt, has looked at the characteristics of over a hundred 'ethnic' minorities in Western Europe alone.

Even where identity is itself fairly simple, it often overlaps, so that parts of Europe are like a microscopic jigsaw of valleys and villages of different nationalities. This complexity has tended to become more simple, given the role of the modern 'nation' state in education and communication. That increase in simplicity may make the principle of self-determination more coherent and applicable, but it does also illustrate that the causal relationship between identity and the state works both ways. In some ways, as the principle suggests, the state with its sovereign independence and defended borders is an expression of the separateness of peoples. To a considerable extent modern Frenchmen, Italians, Germans and Irishmen are a product of the proselytising myths of France, Italy, Germany and Ireland expressed through law, culture and education. In some ways, the imposition of such identities is a restriction of human freedom.

There is, finally, the acute problem of the definition of the relevant territory. Given either a complex identity or an overlapping territory, how should the boundaries be drawn within which the 'self' can determine itself? To take an excessively familiar example, should they be drawn around six counties, or the whole province, or the island or the archipelago?

The central question remains: when Ruritania is freed, in what sense is a Ruritanian a free person? If there is an answer (and this sense of freedom is not a mere extension or analogy), it would seem to be of an essentialist kind. His tribal aspect is freed; he may welcome this personally, but he may not. Many other senses of freedom may suffer as a consequence. Certainly, if Ruritania then passes laws which make education highly religious and nationalistic and bans many kinds of expression and publication, makes economic plans with the consequence that Ruritania stagnates and has no industrial development and makes divorce, abortion and contraception illegal, whereas the Empire was quite tolerant, then we must say that in the primary sense of freedom, Ruritanians have suffered an enormous loss of freedom because Ruritania has been freed.

But, again, the question of national freedom is really one of distinguishing components of the agent from constraints. A sense of national identity can be treated as part of a person, even as the most important or fundamental part, so that no liberty can exist or be worthwhile until it is embodied by a state. Or it can be seen as something imposed upon people from outside, just another inhibition which can be socialised onto the human mind, like religion and class. It depends on how you rank the tribal element in the hierarchy of the soul.

Freedom and education

The relationship between freedom and education is one of the most complex even within the philosophy of freedom. There is an extraordinary tangle of issues and meanings: parents' freedom to determine their children's education and children's freedom within the educational system (which may be in sharp conflict with the freedom of the parents). There is the paradox that education can liberate people from limiting and repressive backgrounds, but that it does so in at least some instances by treating them in an authoritarian manner.

There are three main schools of thought in modern England about the relationship between freedom and education. There are progressive educationalists who take seriously Rousseau's dictum, 'Let us lay it down as an incontrovertible rule that the first impulses of nature are always right.' In different ways the educational methods of A. S. Neill and the 'deschooling' anarchism of Ivan Illich are part of this approach. In general, it argues that children should not be compelled to do anything; facilities for learning should be made available to them, but the demand to learn must come from themselves.

The orthodox liberalism of R. F. Dearden, P. H. Hirst and R. S. Peters takes 'autonomy' as its central concept. One definition of autonomy (Dearden's) has it that 'A person is autonomous to the degree, and it is very much a matter of degree, that what he thinks and does, at least in important areas of his life, is determined by himself.' Educationalists can engage in compulsion, but only on the grounds that they are increasing their pupils' ultimate autonomy.

Finally, the most authoritarian approach (at least in theory) is that of G. H. Bantock and, to some extent, J. P. White. This takes an essentialist view of the agent; compulsion *is* freedom, because it releases the highest and most important of man's capacities, the potential to absorb learning. Bantock says that 'learning matters; and . . . on its maintenance our "true" freedom . . . rests' and 'What the attainment of "true" freedom involves is some measure of restraint: it is, in fact, something to be realised, not something to be accepted.'

None of these approaches is compatible with the breadth and complexity of the concept of freedom. 'Progressive' theory slips into one of two errors. Either it genuinely means that there are no constraints on children to learn, or it does not. If there are none then it is morally and practically wrong: children will not learn on their own, at least not the kind of demanding skills which both pose severe initial difficulties and yet are essential to a high level of intellectual development: mathematics, languages and music, for instance. But what most progressive theorists do is to replace one kind of constraint (a naked sanction such as caning or detention) with others: indoctrination and moral blackmail. It is worth remembering that Rousseau also said of the pupil, 'No doubt he ought only to do what he wants, but he ought to want to do nothing but what you want him to do. He should never take a step you have not foreseen, nor utter a word you could not foretell.'

Nor does 'autonomy' make education and freedom compatible. The idea that we can distinguish which of a person's actions 'are determined by himself' seems merely naive in view of the highly shifting and complex relationship between the idea of a person and that of the constraints upon him. Headmasters since Thomas Arnold have aspired to make their pupils self-regulating along lines chosen by them.

Bantock's own approach can be faulted on grounds of language. In most senses, and certainly in the primary sense of freedom, what we do when we educate children is to curtail their freedom. We make them learn techniques and we do so for many reasons: because they will be more productive, because they will get more satisfaction out of life, so that they can make more money. But, as the Australian philosopher, James Gribble, puts it:

If we lock up children for six or seven hours a day in a school we may free them from their ignorance and give them freedom to engage in activities otherwise inaccessible to them, but insofar as we are constraining people then we are constraining them. . . . It may be unfortunate that there is no necessary connection between 'freedom' and engaging in valuable activities. . . . We do need to justify imposing constraints on children in schools, but an analysis of the concept of 'freedom' does not lead us toward the required justifications.

There can be many justifications for educating people: the most general is that the development of techniques immeasurably enriches people's lives. In some social and cultural contexts it may not be necessary to be authoritarian to achieve education. In others, competing with narrow and anti-educational backgrounds in which only coercion will get a response, it may be necessary to curtail people's freedom in the primary and clearest sense of that word. (I say 'people' because although we normally educate children, it is easy to conceive of circumstances in which the education of adults might be desirable on a non-voluntary basis.) It is the education that matters: the technique is a detail and freedom is, as the song says, just another word.

10

POWER AND ITS
RELATIONS

Two men have an argument about a dog. 'That dog of yours shouldn't be allowed out,' says the first, 'You have no control over it at all.' 'Of course I have,' says the second, 'It's no problem.' 'OK, then, we'll put it to the test,' says the first.

It is relatively easy to design tests which would measure the level of a man's control over a dog. An obvious way of doing it would be to observe its response to a series of commands: 'Sit. Heel. Bite the postman. Don't bite the postman. Fetch the ball. Don't fetch the ball.' The control exercised might not be measurable as a single entity, so that the speed of the animal's response, the range of commands it will obey and the reliability of its response could be viewed separately. It might be possible to achieve a high level of two of these, but not of the other one, in which case the argument about control would not be fully resolved. It might also be possible to estimate the extent to which the dog was controllable and the extent to which the man could control dogs, as well as the existence of control in the relationship between them. The man could be given a variety of dogs (to judge his ability to control) and the dog a number of men (to judge his controllability).

The fundamental criterion of assessing a man's ability to control a dog lies in the inference of a causal relation between his intentions and the dog's behaviour. Clearly we would not be impressed by his claim that he had proved control because the dog was scampering round, barking at everybody and defaecating on neighbours' lawns. He might claim that it only behaved like this because he told it to, but it would be reasonable to suspect that the dog would have behaved like that anyway, whether and whatever commands were given to it. Nor would he have proved anything if we could not understand the relation between command and behaviour: if, for instance, he shouted 'KRP 972' and the dog jumped into the river. The language of command can be anything he chooses or desires: we do not need to understand it to attribute control, but we do need to understand that there is a correlation between his intentions in giving the commands, and the effects achieved; this can only be tested by his getting the dog to do a range of things which he intends, at least some of which the dog was extremely unlikely to do unless commanded. 'Intention' in this context is not quite the same as 'want'; there are senses of 'want' in which the man may not want the dog to obey his command. It may be his dog, and he is calling it to have it taken to the vet to be destroyed, and he wants it to disobey his command and run away, but, in giving the command, he intends it to obey.

The concept of control is relatively straightforward and very widely applicable. We can talk about the extent to which human beings can control entities whether these entities are inanimate or sentient or human. We can talk about a footballer's control over the ball: can he 'make it talk' or 'land it on a sixpence'? Is it 'tied to his bootlaces'? Much of the job of a driving examiner is to assess the extent of people's control over vehicles and the job of the driving instructor is to teach them the means of control. Dressage is a test of a person's control over a horse; sheep–dog trials are more complicated because they measure the effectiveness of a two–stage form of control, man over dog and dog over sheep. In principle there is no difference between these uses of the concept of control and the idea of control over human beings. Most school children, in more traditional schools, at least, operate a fairly precise assessment of the class–control exercised by each teacher. Men joke about the extent to which other men are controlled by their wives, though there is nothing in these jokes to suggest that the assessment is not serious. Chairmen have different levels of control over their companies or university departments, or constituency parties.

It is, though, much more difficult to assess or discuss usefully the control which human beings have over each other, than it is to assess their control over animals and machines. The constituent parts of the operation are likely to vary more confusingly. One man may obey another with a speed and style which suggest a very complete control, but he may be biding his time. Conversely, the speed and style may suggest imminent disobedience, but the grumbler can be 'under the thumb' nevertheless. People are much less predictable; they change their ideas and priorities and, consequently, are less controllable. Human worms 'turn'; real worms remain easier to predict. A large part of the exceptional quality of people as objects of control stems from their self-consciousness. They form images, statements and theories about themselves and, especially, about themselves as the subjects and objects of control, and this makes them dangerously unpredictable. If a man gets a horse to jump a fence seven times, that would constitute very good evidence that he could do so on the eighth time. But a husband who has deferred to his wife on seven previous occasions may well have decided that it is high time he asserted himself. Self-consciousness makes human control over humans much more complicated than other relationships involving control and both self-fulfilling and self-denying analyses may occur. Therefore, statements about control over people furnish much less reliable predictions than statements about control over other entities.

Though it may be difficult to assess one person's control over another we do know what would constitute clear evidence of control. The evidence is less likely to be clear than in other relations and it is much more difficult to devise tests with self-conscious beings. We can even talk about joint control and institutional control to a limited extent. The limitation is on the number of instances in which we can establish a joint or institutionalised intention.

What is the relationship between the concept of control and that of power? Control, on this account, seems to be a relatively simple and straightforward idea, but power has generated an enormous, sophisticated and controversial literature in modern political theory. At the very least, there would seem to be a large overlap between the applications of the two concepts: most cases of control would also seem to qualify, intuitively, as cases of power, and most evidence of the existence of control would seem to constitute evidence of the existence of power. Some theorists have treated the two concepts as if they were, in effect, the same: Bertrand Russell was one of these in that he defined power as 'the production of intended effects'.

But the case of Henry II does not seem to confirm the equation. Henry passed a series of bad-tempered remarks at the dinner table to the effect that genuinely loyal and brave knights would seek to do something about an archbishop who punished bishops for being loyal to the king. As a consequence, four of his knights set off for Canterbury where they murdered the archbishop in question, Thomas Becket. Henry regretted his remarks: he had had (and may have retained) a great personal fondness for Becket and the event severely weakened his political position in Europe and especially in relation to the church. It would seem quite absurd to say that he was in control of the knights as they committed their murder. Indeed, it would be more plausible to say that he was not even in control of himself during his part in the proceedings. But it does seem intuitively correct, even unavoidable, to say that the event was a consequence of the power which Henry possessed.

This problem is resoluble and these two intuitions are compatible with a very close relationship between power and control. Power is the capacity to control. Capacities may not always be used; those who have them may lack the will or the nous to use them. A football commentator may coherently say of a player: 'He has the ability to dominate this game, but he's making no impact at all.' A historian may also say of a political figure: 'He had the power to make enormous changes, but he achieved very little.' Power *is*, therefore, the systematic ability to achieve intentions, despite the opposition of other people, where such opposition exists. But it may have detrimental consequences, even important and frequent ones in the hands of a fool or a blunderer.

The example of Henry II, in the bold terms in which I have described it, could have several interpretations. The knights may have been playing their own game, having their own political reasons for killing Becket. The king's remarks legitimised and made possible their action. Now, it is possible to imagine a king who had no power at all, but whose remarks could be made to justify the intentions of a dominant clique or an *éminence grise*. If he finally stood up for himself and issued independent commands, against their will, they would find some way of getting rid of him. But there might also be a king who had considerable power, but little control. He made blunders like Henry, some of which were seized on by the unscrupulous, some of which were sincerely obeyed, against his will. However, if he could be sober, careful and coherent enough to issue clear commands in line with his intentions, then his will would prevail. Or, he could be a king whose normal degree of

power and control was very large, and the murder was an attempt
to court favour with him. People anticipate the reactions of the
powerful and try to please them; their attempts are not always
successful.

The only way we can distinguish between these possibilities is by
reference to intentions. Whether or not a person has power can only
be resolved as a question of whether he can systematically achieve a
range of intentions and override opponents, irrespective of whether
he does and whether there are instances where his power has un-
intended consequences. This control model of power has very great
conceptual advantages: it allows for the resolution of disagreements
about power and it is firmly based on a concept, control, which has
deep roots in ordinary and practical talk. It is also fully compatible
with the way in which we talk about power in everyday life.

FACES AND DIMENSIONS OF POWER

Readers who are unfamiliar with the modern debate on power
might well think that what I have said so far is elementary and
uncontroversial. But those who are familiar with the debate will
recognise the apparently innocent attempt to define power as a
disguised ideological commitment. For recent theoretical discus-
sions of power, as with those about the closely related subject
of democratic theory, have tended to polarise into two opposed
approaches, one recognisably left-wing and the other, correspond-
ingly, of the right.

Right-wing views of power, of which the most celebrated are
those of Robert Dahl and Nelson Polsby, in both cases in a wide
variety of works, insist that power should be defined clearly and
positively: a good definition is one which can be 'operationalised' in
research projects on particular political structures. Typically it is
defined as the ability to achieve one's intentions against opposition.
The method for the discovery and mapping of power in a particular
context is of detailed examination of what are seen as the most
important decisions and decision-making bodies. By this method
power (in America, at least, but the conclusions can be extended to
include many other Western countries) is found to be highly complex. It is often 'situational', meaning that actors can only affect a

narrow range of decisions in any given period. There are channels of influence which extend to the majority of people in society and the largest concentrations of power are to be found in a number of rival groups rather than in any one group. This implies a relatively kindly portrayal of existing (Western) societies as 'pluralistic' or 'poly-archal'. Very often this view of power is allied with low expectations or standards as to what can be attained in democratic practice, so that the gap between the real and the realistically ideal is fairly small.

The left-wing view is opposite in every respect. It draws on the work of many critical, Marxist, and neo-Marxist sociologists, but it is perhaps best known in political theory through the work of Peter Bachrach, William Connolly and Steven Lukes. Instead of a clear and operational definition of power, many left-wing analyses start with the necessity for a complex and committed understanding of what power is. The mapping of power in a particular society requires, instead of detailed research, the theoretical understanding of the structure and socio-economic nature of that society. Power is discovered to be vested in a class structure; it is the possession of a ruling class or elite. There is an enormous gap between the level of democracy which would be attainable in the best of societies and the working of existing society. Whereas right-wing views start with a fairly simple definition of power and proceed to a highly complex map of the dispersal of power, those of the left begin with a complex insight into power and proceed to a familiar and simple map of society which shows the dominance of one class by another.

There is an important element of the left-wing idea of power which would be difficult to reject. The 'second face' of power which Peter Bachrach and Morton Baratz examined in their essay 'Two Faces of Power' is the ability to prevent opposition being expressed. Suppose a man has a slave. The slave hates the man, but he fears him, and fears the hard beatings that the man gives him, so he is obedient and compliant. This seems as good an example as one can conceive of the power of one man over another. But suppose the man has owned the slave for all of the slave's life and has 'con-ditioned' him so that the slave cannot conceive of disobeying the man and, indeed, his own self-esteem is dependent on the speed and subservience with which he complies with the man's wishes. It would seem odd not to call this power as well; it seems a more complete and reliable form of power than an owner could have over a slave who hates him.

Yet the more 'positive' views of power insist on the existence of opposed intentions before one can talk about power. The example of the slave may seem obscure and extreme, but, like many other examples in political theory, it is used to suggest a logical possibility. It is not difficult to extend the position of the slave to characterise many elements of social control through religion, propaganda, patriotism and education and to see the position of the truly sub-servient slave mirrored in the experience of a deferential lower class.

The control model can absorb the second face of power insofar, and only insofar, as we can meaningfully and truthfully talk about the existence of opposition to the entity which has power and its ability to overcome that opposition. The ownership of a slave, in a society which condones slavery and penalises escape, is surely a relationship of power even in the case of an acquiescent slave who would not choose freedom if it were offered to him because we can say that the master (in league with other masters) *could* forcibly restrain him if he did seek freedom. On the other hand, a purely voluntary slave, in a society which does not recognise slavery and bound only by his own word, presents a very different case. His slavery would seem to rest on his own mental state, whether devotion, inability to cope with choice or whatever, and he could *not* be coerced if he did rebel. It seems more intuitively correct to say that this is not a relationship of power, or that it is very difficult to find out whether it is because we do not know what kind of sanctions, emotional or other, might be applied if he did rebel.

The case of a deferential lower class is less easy to distinguish. Assuming that they form a majority of the society, it seems reason-able to infer at least the possibility that if they had a clear will to overthrow the upper class, they could do so. What constrains them is in their minds, their own values and beliefs. Perhaps some of them want to rebel and are coerced; they see themselves as part of a lower class directly coerced by the upper class. But, in view of the range of attitudes in the society, including those important lower-class attitudes which support the existing social structure, it is more strictly accurate to say that the opposition which exists is between rebels and non-rebels, not between upper and lower classes.

In these circumstances, Bachrach and Baratz talk about the existence of a 'false consensus'; the Marxist idea of 'false conscious-ness' plays a similar role. The idea of *falsehood* is crucial to their argument and it concedes the necessity of opposition before we can talk about power. Only if the consensus or the consciousness is *false* does it make sense to talk of the power of one class over another, most members of which accept the social structure. There must be a sense in which the lower classes are not themselves, some way in which they really are opposed to the social structure without realising it. For it must be at least logically possible, if not sociologically, that the lower classes have a genuine approval of the social structure and that its existence depends on their approval.

At this stage of the argument we are facing the same kind of problems about what counts as an agent as we did when discussing freedom. The deference of the deferential agent can be considered part of himself, or it can be considered as something imposed on him from outside. Treating it as an imposition from outside requires a retreat either to a hypothetical model of that agent or to one which is essential. The proponent of the false consensus view must either say that the agent's view can be treated as genuine only under certain conditions or he must say that he can derive the genuine will of the agent *a priori*. Hypothetical stipulations take two different forms, which differ in very significant ways. Either they say that the agent must be offered certain conditions before his expression of will can be said to be genuine: he must be given a certain amount of information or allowed to hear all points of view. Or they take actual agents as irredeemably corrupt: nothing will bring them to see their true will; they would have seen it in an uncorrupt society, but it is too late now. Essentialist stipulations begin with the premise that men seek autonomy or creativity or God and that any distortion of this search is a falsehood.

There are two classic arguments against this kind of concept of power, as there are against the equivalent and related concepts of freedom and interests. One, a logical argument: they allow for no tests or procedures to resolve arguments. Two, a moral argument: they justify people being made to do things against their will for the peculiarly potent reason that it is not their true will at all.

It seems appropriate at this point to consider an example, not a hypothetical or general example, but a real one and the one most crucial to the arguments of both left- and right-wing theorists of power: the history of the United States of America since 1865. Let us start at the end and work backwards, beginning with the condition of the country in the late twentieth century. The United States now has an overwhelming majority of people who accept its ideology: they are Christian; they believe in individualism, morally, economically and ontologically; they believe in capitalism; they think the American system of government is the only proper one, the best in the world. Their system of belief supports the maintenance of the existing, private ownership of most of the 'means of production' and a consequently inegalitarian distribution of income.

How did this come about? For purposes of argument I am prepared to accept the gist of the socialist social historians' account of events. Since the end of the civil war, America has been controlled by a capitalist elite. They have exercised their control over the means of communication and, particularly since the peak of immigration, over the educational system, to produce a population of believers in the American way of life. Where opposition has been formed they have readily resorted to brutality, slaughtering strikers *en masse* and ensuring the harsh punishment of communist and anarchist opponents of their objectives. They have used the voting system to ensure compliance, overwhelming what opposition remains with their colossal resources. In rare cases, where democratic decisions have gone against them, they have had them overturned by the judiciary. They have at their disposal a systematic and many-headed power.

But they don't need it. The political success of capitalism in America was assured generations ago. Any capacity which the American *haute bourgeoisie* had for unified and organised class repression has long since atrophied as most of their potential enemies have come to support and half-join them. They are no longer the controllers of American society; they are only its beneficiaries. This is a fundamental confusion in many theories of power: clearly, to benefit from something is logically independent of controlling that thing, but many accounts of power talk as if benefit implied control.

So what of the structure of power in American society? Surely, it is dispersed: the system rests on the deep-seated approval of the overwhelming majority. Within that system conflicts of interest are represented by divisions in the game of American politics. It is not true to say that the capitalist class exercises power. That class did exercise power and played a part in ensuring that America was a capitalist country. Hypothetically, if it had not exercised power when it did, America and Americans would be different, possibly even non-capitalist. But to say that the capitalist class exercises power is not a statement about the real America which actually exists. Often, one suspects, it is an essentialist statement based on the premise that the true will of man cannot support capitalism, therefore only a false consensus created by capitalist power can explain the real America.

One of the most essentialist, as well as one of the best known, accounts of power is that in Steven Lukes's *Power: a radical view*. The underlying criterion of all concepts of power, according to Lukes, is that 'A exercises power over B when A affects B in a manner contrary to B's interests.' Lukes says that power has three 'dimensions':

1st: Where there is an observable conflict of policy issues and one side has the capacity to win. This is the sort of power in which Dahl and Polsby are interested.
2nd: Where potential issues are organised out of policy areas and some wants are prevented from expression in the political system: this includes Bachrach's 'second face' of power.
3rd: Where some people's 'real interests' are overridden by the political system even though those people's wants are satisfied.

As an account of power, this breaks conceptual rules in two ways. First, it is not an account of power as we normally talk about it; there is no requirement presupposed by our normal talk of power that the exercise of power should always be against the interests of the person over whom it is exercised. Parents and teachers normally exercise power over children; we cannot assume that it is *always* against the interests of all the children. The second problem concerns the concept of interests. A man's interests can be inferred from an indefinitely large number of accounts of his essence and an indefinitely wide variety of stipulations about the conditions in which he could be said truly to perceive his interests. Arguments between these conceptions of man cannot be resolved: thus Lukes' account of power is not only not an account of power; it also makes it impossible to establish propositions or resolve arguments about power.

Lukes accepts most of these implications. He sees power as a 'fundamentally evaluative' and 'essentially contested' concept, a vehicle, in effect, for the expression of an image of man and of criticism of existing societies. He is, to use a familiar academic catchword, playing a different game from the positivists who want to use the concept to find out how politics in Flatsville or Gotham City really work. I have two major objections to his playing this game. The first is relatively, though not absolutely, trivial; it is that it adds further confusion to the concept of power, a concept which can be quite useful in understanding some political circumstances and events. However, it is only *quite* useful and on *some* occasions. In the real world people are unclear about their intentions, and we never know what matters until long afterwards and perhaps not even then, and we can rarely see what effect any particular agent or set of agents had, with any clarity, so that 'power' seems inappropriate and certainly unmeasurable. Outcomes more closely resemble what C. Wright Mills called the idea of 'history as fate . . . where innumerable decisions add up to a result which no man intended'.

The more important objection is that Lukes is dishonest, perhaps also cowardly. I am not accusing him alone: the charge must also be laid against William Connolly in *The Terms of Political Discourse*, and, on a broader field, against much 'critical' theory and sociology. They are putting moral arguments and offering images of man, but lacing them with so much sociology that it is impossible to disentangle what is recommendation and what observation. If they want to say what the fundamental purposes of men's lives should be or if they want to say, for example, that the means of production ought not to be privately owned, why don't they say so bluntly and allow a clear and overt argument?

Lukes, in effect, announces that he is going to ignore the rules of conceptual analysis and then duly breaks them. The interesting questions are about how he dares to do this and how he gets away with it, for *Power: a radical view* is a very widely quoted and respected book. One reason is that it overlaps with a tradition of *critical* thought (including the occasional Marxist themes of the unity of theory and practice and the primacy of practice over theory) which stress that truth and clarity are either unattainable or trivial and that the objective of talking about society is the propagation of humanist values. These values cannot simply be *argued* in the context of a backward and hostile population: the perceptions of that population must first be transformed by the conviction that it (or a large part of it) is the object of a thoroughly limiting power structure.

The analogy of the three dimensions has considerable rhetorical force. It takes a brave man to say that he favours a two-dimensional view of the world over a three-dimensional view. The argument subtly draws the reader along from what are necessary emendations to the positivist conception into a full-blown 'radical' model. But the most powerful reason for the success of Lukes' argument is that without a model of society in which power creates its own supportive (and 'false') perceptions and values the socialist critique of those capitalist societies in which people can oppose the principles of capitalism without punishment and in which they can vote governments from office, collapses into an unpopular political programme.

THE POWER FAMILY

Returning to the control model of power, there is a certain amount of clearing up to do in respect of the range of terms in the power 'family'.

Coercion, I take it, is the central form of power. It is not stretching a point to say that all cases of power either are cases of coercion or can be established as examples of opinion control and the 'second face' of power. Coercion consists of the use of threats to control someone's actions. It is difficult to define more precisely than that. Is a threat an offer to make someone worse off than they are now, or worse off than they would have been if the threatener had not intervened, or worse off following compliance than following non-compliance? There is a well-founded irony in the expression 'Make him an offer he can't refuse': there is no precise distinction between threats and promises. If my boss suggests that my chances of promotion may largely be dependent on my cooperation with him, is he bribing me with promotion or threatening me with the lack of it? Hillel Steiner's general category of a 'throffer' is a more precise category than the ordinary distinction between threats and bribes (or promises). But threats and promises have very different connotations; insofar as people can distinguish cases in which they are being threatened, coercion is a very central case of power.

Force, on the other hand, is not a form of power if by force is meant the physical control of a person's body. If I drug a girl and put her in the boot of my car and take her to my cellar I control her body. But this physical control is not the same as human control. It may be that she is adamant and unbending; she will not agree to marry me or give me her money or whatever it is I might want. If she is adamant and would rather die than comply, then I control the body, but not the person. If, on the other hand, I can get her to do what I want by threatening her then I do have (coercive) power. But this is logically separate from physical force.

Influence, at least in many of the senses in which the word is normally used, is indistinguishable from power. It is interesting to note that Robert Dahl, sometimes at great pains to distinguish the two, at other times offers the same definition of both. (In *Modern Political Analysis* he says: 'My intuitive idea of power, then, is something like this: A has power over B to the extent that he can get B to do something that B would not otherwise do.' In 'The Concept of Power' he says: 'Our common sense notion, then, goes something like this: A influences B to the extent that he gets B to do something which B would not otherwise do.') Influence is power which is not coercive, but the two cannot be sharply distinguished and there are a great number of important cases which might reasonably be construed as being either. Academic advisors to governments, perhaps the paradigm case of 'influence', are not without some sanctions: they can 'leak' documents, write punitively critical memoirs or change sides.

Persuasion is not a form of power, at least in one of its most familiar and coherent senses. If I persuade somebody to do something I offer him information or reasoning which helps him to see more clearly how to achieve his intentions. There is no requirement that I have any control over him; he can take or leave my advice. Indeed, he may have control over me; I remember persuading a schoolmaster who was at the end of his tether with me that he really ought to give me another chance instead of breaking his own principles on corporal punishment.

'Persuasion' is also used for forms of influence and even coercion; characters in Damon Runyon's stories talk about guns as 'persuaders'. It is sometimes difficult to distinguish from manipulation, by which a person's intentions are modified, distorted or replaced by the persuader in his own interests. In all of these senses, though not in its central sense, persuasion is a form of power.

Liberty is related to power in important ways; many statements about liberty imply statements about power and vice versa. But there is no straightforward or symmetrical relationship between the two concepts. One man or a group of men could have considerable power in a society, but the general level of liberty could still be high if, for example, the rulers had libertarian principles. In a society of rigidly accepted and enforced rules it would be possible that a man be deprived of his liberty without anybody having power over him because nobody had any choices in their treatment of him. (A kind of parallel to the headmasterly 'This is going to hurt me more than it is going to hurt you.') A sense of unfreedom is often combined with a sense of powerlessness and a sense of being oppressed, but the existence of these senses does not imply that there is anyone who has the power, any more than the existence of the desire to pray implies that there is a God.

Authority is logically separate from power. It consists of rights to command and corresponding duties to obey. Like property, authority is a concept of the rights 'family' and it can be talked about in quite different ways. A man living in a nationalist area of Northern Ireland is legally subject to the authority of the United Kingdom. But that authority might only be minimally accepted and the IRA might have authority within the community. Yet the man himself might say that he recognises no authority except God, or an all-Ireland socialist republic or a Jacobite king.

All talk of authority implies some kind of acceptance, though this acceptance is not necessarily the acceptance of the person over whom authority is exercised at any one time. The prisoner may say, as a critical account of the proceedings, 'I do not recognise the authority of this court.' But the judge can offer a rather more important mode of talking about authority and reply, in effect, 'I sentence you using the authority vested in me by the Queen-in-Parliament, which is accepted as the sovereign body of this state, which is recognised by all other states in the world.'

Although authority is logically separate from power, possession of the two often coincides. One of the reasons why this happens is that authority can be causally related to power: it can be one of the resources, like money, status and force, on which power can be based. But in modern and complex societies of the sort Max Weber typified as 'rational-legal' and 'bureaucratic', authority is often very difficult to convert into power. The man behind the social security desk may snub you and keep you waiting, but there is little else he can do at your expense. The judge may send you to prison, but if he then makes approaches to your wife he could be in a lot of trouble. Authority in modern societies is defined and constrained by precise roles and generates relatively little power.

Authority and power may be causally related to a third factor, such as parenthood. Being a parent normally gives people both power and authority over their children. The authority usually outlives the power, at least in the stronger senses of the word power.

CONCLUSION

For all the complexities of power and related concepts, analyses of what power is come down to one of two things. Either they are attempts to clarify our talk about how things actually happen or they are attempts to change society by persuading people that their existing attitudes and values are not their true views because they are the consequences of a social power structure. In either case, a political programme which claimed to achieve a 'redistribution of power' cannot be taken seriously. Either the proposal is obscure and trivial, or it represents a disguised programme to impose upon people values and beliefs which are, by the very nature of the theory, opposed to the values and beliefs which they consciously hold.

11

FORMS OF GOVERNMENT

Traditionally, political philosophy has concerned itself with the virtues and defects of various forms of government. The list of such forms is potentially endless to anyone who possesses a Greek dictionary: monarchy, autocracy, democracy, aristocracy, theocracy, isocracy. . . . All of these words purport to label a particular form of rule: by one man, by priests, by a hereditary group, by all the citizens or whatever. The making of such taxonomies of government is by its nature a fairly crude exercise. Much more complex prescriptions for the form government should take can be found in the works of such political philosophers as Hobbes, Locke and Rousseau. Their theories contain a series of inferences from the nature and circumstances of man to the details of the form which government should take.

It is fair to say that political philosophy of this kind is outdated and that it has been considerably undermined by political science. Categories of government do not catch the subtle but vastly significant variations of real politics; inferences about the best forms of government seem foolishly abstract in the context of the wonderfully wide variety of local political conditions which exist in the late twentieth century. Even if one were to regard one of the contemporary political philosophers of the old style, perhaps John Rawls or Robert Nozick, as ultimately correct, it would be difficult to know how to interpret their work in the immediate context of Northern Ireland or Zimbabwe or Belgium.

The form of government, in its most formal sense, is not very important. Up to about 1914 it seemed to be very important. But in

1914 the world was dominated by a handful of great empires, the administration of which bore little relation to the prescriptions of any political philosopher. Although there were exceptions, most notably in France and the United States, for the most part it could be said that the schemes of political philosophers had gone untested. But now the evidence is much more considerable; over 100 states have been established in the period since 1918, mainly on liberal or on Marxist principles, and the range of evidence allowing the comparison of theory with practice is vastly greater.

This large body of evidence has supported the limited evidence which was available before, and together they suggest a proposition which is as close to being a law of politics as the subject can provide: forms of government adapt to suit the people who operate them. Montesquieu, not alone among political theorists in his admiration for the British system of government, diagnosed that the significant feature of that system was the separation of the powers of the legislature and the executive and the consequent existence of a series of checks and balances which served as constraints on any immoderation by governments. It was partly under his influence that the American constitution formalised the separation of powers which evolved into the very different system of government, the constrained presidency, which is special to the United States. Meanwhile, British government was changing as the institutions of prime minister and cabinet evolved and took over most of what we would now call the policy-making functions of the executive from the monarchy. A century after Montesquieu the 'efficient secret' (as Bagehot was later to call it) of British government was being observed to be the very opposite of the separation of powers: the combined power over executive and legislature which lay in the cabinet, this power being spearheaded by the executive's ability to dissolve the legislature. The drafters of the constitution of the Third French Republic attempted to imitate this feature, but it fell into abeyance and the government of France continued to work in very different ways from that of Britain.

Abstract constitutional principles generally meet one of two fates. They can simply fail to take root (to employ the old analogy of botany and politics), in which case they are either ignored and become dead letters or they are casually discarded. Or they can become the formal shell and legitimation of forms of government quite different from the authors' intentions. The Soviet Union provides examples of both. Insofar as it is a 'dictatorship of the proletariat' drawing on Marx and 'Marxist' writing (especially Lenin's *State and Revolution*) for its principles of government, it has worked quite differently from the ways in which most of its intellectual supporters would have intended. Whether it is much different from what either Marx or Lenin in certain moods would have expected is a matter of exigesis beyond the scope of this book. But no Marxist theory, reasonably interpreted, can properly be said to justify the existence of a powerful state bureaucracy dominated by a narrow party elite for many decades. Even so, Marxist theory provides the definition and self-justification of this government. At the same time, the Soviet state has been defined by a constitution (the 1936 'Stalin' constitution) which is largely liberal in content, which asserts the rights of individuals and the necessity of the rule of law, stipulations which turn out to be dead letters in the crucial hard cases when the regime considers that its status is in jeopardy.

Constitutional law and principle have been taken more seriously in the United States of America than anywhere else. But even there a strong tendency for abstract principles to mould themselves to suit powerful political forces has been manifest. Under the American constitution all citizens are equal and endowed with certain fundamental rights, but slavery persisted under that constitution for the best part of a century. Toleration of belief and freedom of expression are principles of that constitution, but that did not prevent the House of Representatives Un-American Activities Committee from persecuting people who were sympathetic to Marxism in the 1950s.

The largest single category of constitutions which have withered away have been those in ex-British colonies. A few have simply worked very differently from what was anticipated: Zambia, Singapore and Malawi have been, in effect, autocracies. But many more have been dropped in favour of military dictatorship, the whole 'Westminster model' with its fine detail of wigs and maces and legislative procedures being superseded by a form of government which England abandoned in 1660.

Political science offers two kinds of theory to explain the failure or irrelevance of constitutional principles. But the two, though different in emphasis, are not incompatible. There are, first, theories of the determinant effects of social and economic relations on political institutions. There is a strong tendency for these theories to become or to support developmental theories which emphasise political 'maturity' and 'modernity'. Very often, especially in American hands, an important emphasis of such theories is that a relatively high level of economic development is a necessary condition of the persistence of sophisticated legal and electoral systems and high levels of individual freedom. But there are also theories of political culture: these emphasise the widely varying content of norms, values, myths and beliefs in different contexts, and the localness of nations, states, societies and languages. The implication of theories of culture is that it may matter more whether a society is 'Latin' or 'Anglo-Saxon' than whether it has a high or a low level of economic development.

However, although the emphasis of a developmental theorist like Barrington Moore is very different from that of a cultural one like Gabriel Almond, their accounts of politics are not necessarily incompatible. Developmental theories override and sometimes ignore local differences without having to deny them. Economic development can sometimes affect the attitudes to which 'culture' refers; the reverse can also happen. Which of these is normally cause and which normally effect has been highly controversial, especially in the case of accounts of the early development of capitalism.

But it does not matter to my argument whether capitalism led to protestantism or vice versa. The two kinds of theory suggest many similar propositions about constitutions and formal principles of government. They suggest that the institution of a rule may not be compatible with people's basic norms and beliefs and that these are very hard to change. Liberal laws and institutions cannot easily be superimposed on an authoritarian society. The integrity of the state and the legal system has to struggle with tribalism. Universal suffrage does not work the same way in an atmosphere of elitism and fatalism as it does in bourgeois Switzerland. The expectation of corruption undermines all formal political procedures.

These observations in themselves amount to a kind of conservative law; they suggest that government cannot be made over on first principles without very great coercion or patience or both. But it is a very promiscuous conservative principle, one that could be cited to support Stalin and the Ayatollah Khomeini as easily as the British monarchy. Nor does it suggest any clear prescriptions: however difficult it may be to impose constitutional principles on a corrupt society, it is not necessarily wrong to try.

So far I have been talking about forms of government in a very formal sense, as defined by their constitutional principles, normally written principles. At this level of formality America is a bicameral federal presidential system and Sweden a unicameral constitutional monarchy. There are much less formal ways of classifying government – as 'capitalist', 'corporatist', 'consociational', 'prime ministerial', 'decentralised', 'polyarchal' or 'tribal'. The advantage of such informal categories over formal constitutional distinctions is that they can get much closer to grouping governments according to the spirit in which they actually work. But the disadvantage is that such forms cannot be clearly prescribed and discussed. It is empty to suggest that government should be 'decentralised' or 'corporatist' or 'consociational'; such statements are not recommendations until they are translated into formal constitutional arrangements applicable to particular circumstances. And for all the cultural, social and economic constraints on the working of formal principles, nobody could seriously suggest that they do not have real effects. The actual content, the working, of the American constitution has affected the course of American history at times, however plastic that constitution has been at other times under the pressure of real political power. Nobody could seriously deny that the introduction of some form of proportional representation would radically affect the reality, and even the cultural context, of British politics. But the real consequences of changes of form are difficult to discern in advance and rarely what their authors intend. Anyone who wished to be serious about proportional representation in Britain would need to study its consequences in such countries as Israel, the Netherlands, the Republic of Ireland and the Federal Republic of Germany and then to speculate as to which of those consequences would obtain in Britain and evaluate the probabilities and related alternatives.

SOME BAD FORMS OF GOVERNMENT

A number of words suggest forms of government of which it is conventional to disapprove. Autocracy suggests the formal rule of one man, dictatorship a reality which amounts to the same thing. There can, though, be collective dictatorships by small and inaccessible groups. Tyranny is a highly emotive term, best defined by other emotive terms such as brutality, oppression and arbitrary power. The twentieth century has added to the taxonomy of undesirable governance the term 'totalitarianism'. This word was popularised by Mussolini in Italy in the 1920s, but the concept of totalitarianism has been further developed in Western political science in the 1950s by such writers as Carl Friedrich, Zbigniew Brzezinski and Hannah Arendt. The kind of model of government which tended to emerge out of these writings was, perhaps, too specific. Totalitarianism was defined (especially by Brzezinski and Friedrich) in terms of a wide range of conditions which included the domination by a single leader, a mass party, methods of terror, the eradication of all power bases from the state and the party, and a secret police force. The logical error lay in putting too many properties into a definition, with the consequence that, if the Soviet Union was totalitarian under Stalin, it was no longer so by the 1960s because leadership had begun to take a very different role (and one which involved the peaceful and legal replacement of a supreme leader) and terror, at least in the sense in which it had existed during the French revolution or under Stalin, was no longer used. For that matter, Mussolini himself seems a poor totalitarian, given the continued existence of such alternative power bases as the Church and the carabinieri and his own replacement even within the Fascist party. Totalitarianism seems so weak in retrospect that one is obliged to conclude that much of the appeal of the concept came not only from the general academic desire to categorise, but also from the propaganda value of a category of government which associated Soviet Russia with fascist Italy and Nazi Germany. The Russians were, naturally, quite prepared to reciprocate, their categories of 'reactionary' and 'imperialist' governments (and sometimes 'fascist' as well) tarring America with the same brush as the regimes of Hitler and Mussolini. For that matter, one could easily cook up a category of government which associated America and Russia with each other, as megalithic governments obsessed with security and military domination, each constrained by a rigid and solemn conception of its own 'way of life'.

However, there is something about at least some of the regimes which have been described as totalitarian which it is important to distinguish from mere tyrannies, dictatorships and despotisms. Caligula was a tyrant, a dictator and a despot, but the great bulk of the vast empire which he ruled lived on in ignorance of him.

Caligula's objectives were trivial. According to Suetonius, he was 'interested only in doing the apparently impossible', whether it was driving tunnels under the sea or sleeping with all the most beautiful people in Rome. He killed many people, some of them very brutally, on no systematic grounds, but on mere whim. Frederick the Great was an autocrat, but he did not interfere with his people's lives and ideas except so far as it was necessary for his military adventures.

But some regimes in the twentieth century have taken a more thorough interest in the affairs and minds of their citizens than almost any previous governments, so that art and science and even love have been added to religion and politics as subjects upon which the state prescribes uniquely acceptable opinions. The most extreme cases have come under Stalin in the 1930s (before war made it politic to be more tolerant and broadly nationalist) and under Mao's 'cultural revolution'. In these cases the state had an official view of virtually everything and was prepared to back its view with coercive sanctions. The state enforced an intellectual *weltanschauung* or world-scheme; I think it is necessary to avoid using the word 'ideology' in this context, as it has been used in too many diverse and contentious ways. This is surely the new and terrifying feature of twentieth-century government and it is one which has moved such writers as Orwell and Koestler and Wells to fear and anger.

Roughly one can arrange governments along a continuum, according to the answers that can be given to the questions, 'How much do they tolerate?' and 'What range of subjects do they consider relevant to their legitimacy?' and, perhaps, 'How wide is the range of opinions which a person can express and still be a part of the government?' At one extreme of the continuum would be the more orthodox Marxist-Leninist regimes in which a person could only come into government by passing, in effect, tests of correctness on religion, art, physics, biology and other subjects. At the other end would be, perhaps, Harold Wilson's Labour cabinet of 1964–70, a self-styled 'pragmatic' form of government in which cabinet members could be Catholic or atheist, philistine or artistic, modernist or traditional, and believe virtually anything they chose about philosophy or science. Somewhere in between would be Ronald Reagan's Republican government in America.

In other words, there is much to be said for a limited concept of totalitarianism something like an important part of Hannah Arendt's theory which stresses the *totality* of totalitarianism rather than its particular institutional forms and methods. The totalitarian outlook turns everything into politics, makes the legitimacy of government depend on orthodoxy in all fields and thus opens the possibility of the most comprehensive crushing of people's creative and intellectual capacities. But 'totalitarian' in this sense is not so much a formal category of government as an aspect of the life of the mind controlled by complex forces which, though not beyond the control of man, are beyond stipulation by precise formulae. Totalitarianism is bad and should be avoided, but that is to be done by judgement and courage and a sense of humour rather than by political theory.

THE UNIVERSAL PANACEA OF GOVERNMENT

Since 1945 for the first time in the history of ideas a form of government has existed which has had the approval of the overwhelming majority of the world's politicians and intellectuals. Or, at least, there has been a name for forms of government which has had such approval. I refer, of course, to 'democracy', that form of government of which Greece claims to be the mother, Britain the modern guardian, America the defender and Russia the reality. The word 'democracy' has become a pure example of what the American philosopher C. L. Stevenson called a 'dynamic' meaning; that is, one which expresses an emotive attitude to the object to which it is applied. Its descriptive meaning, the clear and widely held rules and conventions governing the proper use of the term, is non-existent.

To favour democracy is empty and pious unless one can establish that one's own precise explication of the concept can claim to be the real one and all the others false. Frankly, I do not think that this is possible and, therefore, serious discussion about democracy as such is not possible. The literal meaning of the word, 'the rule of the people', is no meaning at all. We are all people. The making of policy has to be delegated to somebody. But whom? How chosen? On what terms? For how long? How are they answerable? How do you qualify to be one of them? These are the important questions, 'democracy' merely a container vessel for them. The model, or 'original exemplar' as believers in essentially contested concepts would call it, of democracy, was ancient Athens. But it is a model which is neither easily translatable into modern terms nor especially admirable in itself. The 'democracy' of Athens disenfranchised most of its inhabitants, was generally dominated by demagogues, made very bad decisions (like invading Sicily even though 'nobody knew where it was' as Thucydides put it) and did not last very long. This is quite apart from the fact that Attica was small, sunny, had a simple but stable economy and had no real need of internal policy except for a code of criminal and civil law.

Democracy can be broken down into constituent variables: popular sovereignty (government of the people) and public participation (government by the people). But there are many good reasons for suggesting that welfare and participation can be related conversely. Some of these will be suggested below, but mathematicians since the Marquis de Condorcet in the eighteenth century have demonstrated that even in relatively simple situations with small numbers of rational and fully informed persons, the full and equal participation of everybody in the making of decisions does not necessarily produce as 'good' a result in terms of the general satisfaction of wants as do less directly participatory rules of decision.

In Britain, it is often difficult to believe that even the most enthusiastic theoretical proponents of democracy mean very much by their support. Often they shrink away in practice even from simple and well-tried methods of linking government decisions more directly to public opinion such as referenda and ballots, proportional representation and primary elections. Much political debate about democracy is a mere rhetorical competition. Everybody favours 'democracy' in the abstract, but very few favour the direct rule of public opinion even when it appears to agree with them.

This is not to say that the whole vast literature of democratic theory is just so many wasted words, based on a mistake. Much modern writing in the area focuses on the concept of participation and deals with interesting practical and moral questions: How can people participate? In what fields? With what effects? Since the 1960s these questions have been a major source of academic political controversy: one bibliography covering aspects of public participation in environmental planning, and dealing with works published only in the English language, and mainly in England, between 1968 and 1978, covered over 100 pages.

The proponents of participation have redeveloped a number of arguments which were earlier developed in nineteenth-century political theory, in the writings of John Stuart Mill in particular. A participatory society has three kinds of advantage over one which is passive or deferential. It produces better decisions; *ceteris paribus*, the more people whose knowledge and interests inform a policy, the more in the public interest it is likely to be. Secondly, the quality of social and political relations is improved by higher participation: society as a whole becomes more communal and there is a greater sense of involvement and commitment. Finally, the advantage which in many theories is taken to be of more importance than the others: political participation is both necessary and sufficient for a high level of personal development. Fully rounded, fully human, people can mature only in a social system in which they can exercise a collective control of the conditions governing their own lives. In those societies (that is, most societies) in which people do not freely and collectively participate in the institutions which govern their lives, they can be said to be stunted in growth.

There are many counter-arguments. The *ceteris paribus* assumption which suggests that greater participation produces greater welfare has little relation to reality. In most societies the condition of limited, 'representative' government is such that a small proportion of people participate in the making of policy beyond casting a vote. Let us say that the figure for 'representative' government is normally 2 per cent. Then an attempt is made to open decision-making to more 'participatory' institutions, public meetings, open fora, systems of workers' and neighbourhood committees, detailed surveys of opinion. All these things involve time and effort and expertise. In practice this limits participation to those with certain resources (largely, though not entirely, the educated middle classes). So 'participation' rises from 2 per cent to, perhaps, 10 per cent: rarely more for any extended involvement. There is no reason to suppose that the 10 per cent is more representative of the 100 per cent than was the 2 per cent. In fact there is every reason to suspect that it will be less so, for the 2 per cent were 'professional' politicians: they were, at least, visible and accountable. In the old system the chief executive could say, 'We did it because . . .' and stand responsible for his decisions. In the new one he can only say, 'That was the policy which emerged from the procedures. You should have come to the meeting.' (This abstract account mirrors, in many respects, the experience of increase in participation in English environmental planning since 1968.)   —

All of the arguments for participation have their opposites. Participation costs time and effort; the resulting 'politicisation' can cause social relations to become more bitter and fractious as easily as it can improve them. When viewed in the light of real, humdrum politics, does not the argument for self-development seem fanciful? Is sitting on committees and working out budgets and addressing meetings so much more creative, educative and humane than poetry, love, gardening or cricket? Each of them has costs in terms of the other: time, emotional commitment and the capacity for learning are limited resources.

Like all good arguments, this one is irresoluble. Conservatives can always point to the unsatisfactory reality of participation, radicals can insist that it takes time to develop a participatory society and that such development has to break through habit and tradition and the self-fulfilling prophecies of a deferential society. Then conservatives can reply, even if they admit the desirability of the participatory society as such, that it is difficult to see how it can be achieved at all and more than difficult to imagine it happening without immense cost and disruption.

I do not think that the conservative case need depend on such speculative arguments about what can or cannot be achieved in the way of social change. There is a far more fundamental weakness in the radical case for participation and it concerns something which I have so far allowed to be taken for granted: the concept itself. 'Participation' is, in its logical properties, similar to 'action' and 'production', and a great deal more complex than it appears. The distinction on which it is based would appear to be clear and well established: we know how to tell those who are participating in an activity from those who are not. This works well enough for football and fishing and sex, but there are a number of social activities, including politics, in which the distinction is a great deal more difficult and, even, ultimately impossible to make.

There are a number of ways in which one can appear to play a part in politics but, in a very real sense, not be said to participate in political decisions at all. One can be on the losing side of the political struggle, perhaps never having had a chance and making no difference at all in the final outcome. In such circumstances the loser can talk to his heart's content, but he cannot be said to have played a part in the *decision* or *policy*. What part did the 'nationalist community' play in the Stormont regime in Northern Ireland? How often do the Opposition play a part in the decisions of the House of Commons? These seem particularly simple examples of what is often a complex and disguised truth, that losers cannot really be said to have influenced or participated in the decisions which defeated them.

Then there is the case of people participating in a decision where the choice is forced by circumstances beyond their control. An interesting case of this is the idea of 'workers' control' of industry in competitive market conditions: the decision can be a formality because commercial constraints dictate what must be done. Mrs Margaret Thatcher, as leader of the Opposition, visited Yugoslavia in December 1977 and commented that the systems of workers' control there was in many respects more efficient than British industry because in Yugoslavia workers were forced to face up to reality. In many cases Yugoslav workers in the once-fashionable system of 'workers' control' have delegated their powers to experienced West German managers in order to keep their jobs or hold the purchasing power of their wages. In Mrs Thatcher's terms, the 'reality' of the market deprives the participant of his power.

Mere presence is not participation. Sitting and listening to Pericles or the president of the Students' Union or following the unanimity of the mass meeting because everybody knows what the result will be is no more 'participation' than watching political programmes on television is participation. But there is no easy distinction in politics between mere presence and genuine participation: such a distinction can only hang on the most complex of relations, the true state of liberty and power in a particular circumstance. In that sense, politics is not at all like fishing or football.

Mere consultation does not count as participation. If the boss comes round the mill and says, 'How's it going, Higginthwaite?', and asks you for any suggestions for improvements, and you tell him that if he shortens the lunch hour and lengthens the tea break he'll get more work out of the women, you are not participating. He has the power, he makes the decisions; you are merely a source of ideas and information. He only has to listen on his own terms, as would become clear if you advised him to give the mill to a workers' cooperative.

In short, there are two kinds of conservative objection to increasing participation which should, by now, be familiar in their logical shape: participation is something of a chimera and attempts to increase it can be costly and dangerous. But, once again, flexibility must be the only firm principle. In certain circumstances, when a demand arises, increasing participation may be necessary to preserve stability. Sometimes, it actually does improve the quality of decisions. The increase in public participation in English environmental planning since 1968, for all that it is 'elitist' and does not confirm the arguments of democratic theory, has been a good thing. It has brought more sources of information and ideas to bear on decisions and has helped to counter-balance the bias in favour of growth and development which existed in the (equally elitist) system before 1968.

SENSIBLE GOVERNMENT

So what kind of government am I recommending? My answer, cautious but, I hope, canny, borrows terms which were familiar in eighteenth-century political theory: government which is mixed and moderate and suitable to local conditions.

The popular element in mixed government seems generally necessary: elections (meaning reasonably open and genuinely competitive elections) are a good idea, if not always, then nearly always, at least in 'developed' countries. The electoral element should include such 'participation' as is consistently demanded and which can be incorporated with the other elements of government. These activities make government legitimate; that is, they offer a mechanism for the removal of wildly unpopular and unsuccessful regimes, and they channel political energies into forms of action which can be seen as 'inside' the constitution rather than 'outside' it. These effects generally outweigh the rather obvious disadvantages of elections: they can bring to power untrained leaders incapable of considerations which move beyond the short-term and obsessed with electoral victory. But not always; having had the unusual experience of teaching political philosophy to someone who had led a military *coup d'état* in one of the world's largest countries about a decade before, I am prepared to acknowledge that there can be circumstances in which military or one-party government is the best temporary expedient.

Government should also include a professional element, a body of people who bring it continuity, whose self-esteem is dependent on being able to play a part in policy-making which is honest and expert and orientated towards the long-term. Professionals can also be specialists in a way that politicians cannot. A dignified element, in the sense that Bagehot described it, is also necessary. There should be aspects of government which embody the people's traditions and their sense of nationality, which frame the state in glory and grandeur and glamour and which attract the love and loyalty of the people. These should not, of course, be the same institutions as attract conflict and unpopularity by actually making decisions!

There are many advantages to a hereditary element in government. It offers a source of leadership which is neither socially ambitious nor socially mobile. Hereditary heads of state provide the most effective of dignified elements; there is no substitute, in dignity and in glamour, for the monarch who was *born* to his position and whose family history is intertwined with that of the nation over many generations. Hereditary monarchy and aristrocracy cannot really be rationally defended in an age whose assumptions are secular and egalitarian. That is one of their strengths. Because they cannot really be defended, the hereditary aspect of government manages to be, simultaneously, both wonderful and risible; it inspires devotion, but cannot, by its very nature, inspire fanaticism. Monarchy partly immunises the body politic against ideological disease.

A hereditary and dignified element of government produces people who are not successes, but phenomena; there is no need for envy of their position and no reason for ambition to aspire to it. Formal acknowledgement of hereditary authority takes adulation away from politicians. More than that, it serves to contradict the debilitating pretence that life is 'fair' or people 'equal' and that everybody can 'succeed' or should try to. After all, real power and privilege and wealth are partly hereditary everywhere, in the Soviet Union and the United States and the Republic of Ireland, just as much as in Britain.

This account of mixed and moderate government is, of course, a defence of the British constitution and the British monarchy. It is not the only possible defence of the monarchy: more local arguments can be mounted that the monarchy is a necessary condition of the multi-national nature of the state and that, in the absence of the monarch, the state would have to attempt the difficult, divisive and dangerous business of devising a proper constitution. Nor is it a prescription that British constitutional monarchy should be the universal form of government; it would work quite differently in a different context. But my account does imply approval of the British form of government as one of the few which contains all the elements necessary for good government. That Britain is thought of as a 'failure' both by many of its inhabitants and by many outside commentators seems to me to be a considerable exaggeration of its defects which are, in any case, not the fault of its constitution.

12

THE MEANING AND
PURPOSE OF LIFE

Contemplating the meaning of life is neither a preoccupation nor a high priority for conservatives whose political beliefs are more orientated towards avoiding disaster. Scepticism and pessimism are the important points; disbelief rather than belief has been the emphasis of this book, as it is of conservatism in general. Beliefs and ends, religion and fox-hunting, are often considered by conservatives to be matters for private concern rather than public argument.

Even so, it is reasonable to ask of any social or political philosopher what stands as the end or purpose of his argument. He ought to attempt the questions 'What's it all about?', 'What is life for?', 'What makes life worth living?' It cannot be about balancing the budget or regulating the market mechanism or the maintenance of social order, which are the subjects of much intellectual effort by conservatives. Nor can it be about establishing that 'right' or 'equality' or 'justice' are mere words, rather than coherent ideals, which has been the major theme of this book. These are the means, but what are the ends?

Of course, there is no absolute or external purpose to life. 'Purpose' exists only in a context, like 'need'. 'Meaning' exists only in minds which can perceive events and endow them with value and understanding. Meaning and purpose are mental concepts: answers to questions about them must be either in one's own mind or in the mind of God; they cannot lie in the inanimate forms of the universe itself. Since there is no reliable or agreed procedure for discovering the contents of the mind of God, the answers must lie in ourselves, even if God appears as part of them. Thus in an important sense the idea of a meaning or purpose to life is nonsense. In modern England, the expression 'the meaning of life' is most often used in a humorous context. The meaning is said to be '42' or 'a lemon'; the joke trades on an intuitive understanding of the absurdity of the concept. In a final and scientific sense of truth, it is true that one's own life is a chemical accident, to be interpreted by one's own lights.

It might be thought that the remaining answers were no answers at all. Rape, religion and revolution all give meaning and purpose to people's lives. Is there no standard by which they can be judged? The *sense* of satisfaction in life may well be a consequence of chemistry in its strict sense. My own sense of satisfaction has always been unreasonably high; that of many other people has often seemed to me to be inappropriately low.

But there are, I think, general and public questions which can be asked about human activities and the meaning and purpose which they give to life, and there are criteria which are implied by those questions. We can ask questions about the breadth of the satisfaction arising from activities: can they be spread among and shared by a majority of people? There are questions, too, about the length and depth of satisfaction which activities can generate and about how complete and durable satisfaction is.

The word 'satisfaction' has entered this argument, as if I have tacitly assumed that all questions about the meaning or purpose of life collapse automatically into questions about the satisfaction that life can give. Is this not a controversial utilitarian assumption which will only appeal to Benthamites? The answer, I think, is both 'Yes' and 'No'. In the absence of God, natural law and duty (that is, a rationally deducible code of duty) questions about the meaning or purpose of life can only be answered in terms of the satisfaction which can be achieved in life. To proceed on the assumption of those absences is undoubtedly Benthamite, because Jeremy Bentham was a most impressive conceptual sceptic who devoted a considerable part of his intellectual efforts to demonstrating that the concepts of God, duty, natural law and natural rights lacked coherence and moral force. But Bentham then went on to construct a moral philosophy based on pleasure which assumed that everyone does, as a matter of fact, always seek pleasure and that there is an overall aggregate of pleasure in society which legislators can be called upon to maximise. Those propositions are not true; they are false or incoherent depending on how one interprets them.

Bentham's 'calculus' of pleasure with its multiplicative computations of 'felicity' and 'fecundity' and 'duration' is as great a nonsense on stilts as that which he so effectively attacked. So what we are left with is satisfaction, not in any precise or quantifiable sense, but as a general word for the mental states which might count as ends once the idea of a grand design to the universe has been rejected. It is a covering word, nothing more. If it is a 'concept' at all, it is many-headed, multi-dimensional, but it is a word which gets nearer to covering the criteria of coherent purposes in life than any other.

These general criteria, considered in the light of experience and in the context of the nature of human life, suggest certain general principles of satisfaction. The greatest of human satisfactions are those which root a person to his own time and place. It matters that objectives can be attained. It is also important that they can be shared: a purely personal pleasure can have no great depth. But attainment should not be easy; there is no real satisfaction in doing something which comes easily. The deepest satisfaction comes from those things which require hard work and the development of technique. Risk is also important; no achievement or possession is of much value unless it required risk in the attainment. Winning is of no value unless you might have lost. 'Taking things for granted' is perhaps the commonest mistake that people make about their own interests. They assume that what they already have is guaranteed and, therefore, trivial and become obsessed with what they lack, by the next stage in their plan for their own development. Most people, most of the time, are not satisfied with life: they pine for something extra. 'If only I could have . . . a wife, promotion, a new car, my own house, a son . . .': this is the commonest way in which people think about their interests.

Only one thing can be enjoyed without risk and that is the past. For that reason, satisfaction can be achieved only by activities which are partly discrete, which offer completions and new beginnings. Games are won and lost, harvests gathered in and consumed, performances are ended and the applause dies down.

By these criteria, and talking generally, what does not seem to provide genuine satisfaction in life is the pursuit of abstract states such as 'fame', 'success', 'socialism' and 'wealth'. If anything, these are means; as ends, they have a tragic intangibility. Like the rainbow's end, they are not really there when you arrive.

By contrast, there are certain satisfactions which are more 'real' in the sense of being deep and abiding and unchanging. There is allegiance, the sense of belonging, the lump in the throat on the crest of the hill when you know you are nearly home. Allegiance can be to an area, a town, a country or to a set of boundaries of one's own devising. It can be to an entity as large as a nation or to one as small as a household. It tends to be excessively abstract applied to large entities, but is fragile in relation to small ones. Patriotism is, perhaps, the most important form of allegiance. Dr Johnson said that it was 'the last refuge of the scoundrel' but, being a philosophical ignoramus, he did not distinguish between the love of one's country (which is the normal sense of patriotism) and support for a state which overrides all other moral judgements. There is nothing wrong with patriotism in the simple sense: it is an emotion, not a moral position, and those who lack it, not those who express it, should be suspected, but not pre-judged, of being scoundrels.

One aspect of allegiance is a relationship to land, a sense of belonging to the land and of it being one's own in a way that transcends the contingencies of ownership. Exploring it, digging it, growing things on it, looking at it, smelling it: the sense of being part of the earth, which William Morris and many other critics of urban and industrial society thought was lost to man, is one of the deepest pleasures. One ancient aspect of it is ownership, the husbandry of one's own patch. One modern aspect is preservation, the endless struggle to protect land and plants and buildings from 'development' or, at least, to slow down the rate of change.

Creation is a real and fundamental satisfaction: the making of things which can be consumed. The scale of modern industry often leaves man without a product; not surprisingly, he tends to retreat from it when he can, to the garden, the university or to socialism. There is immense satisfaction too, in technique: in doing things simply because they are difficult, so that the process and not the product becomes the end. Also in charity, not in the Kantian sense of duty nor in the socialist sense of a compulsory redistribution of resources, but in the broad sense of doing things for other people without needing or bothering to distinguish whether what one does is ultimately selfish or altruistic. And the dynastic pleasures, revering ancestors, educating sons and daughters and the clear realisation of oneself as a link in a vast genetic chain: this is part of the sense of one's own identity. There is also deep satisfaction in competition, especially when there are fair rules.

This is not a list of my own tastes and prejudices. I am attempting to categorise the most important kinds of human pleasures and satisfactions, those which give the fullest meaning to life. In doing so, I am likely to cause both anger and laughter, since I am discussing something which is a taboo subject for much modern (liberal) thought because such thought insists that what people do in their 'spare' time is a matter of 'taste' and not a proper subject for philosophical and social theorising. The autonomy of choice being equal, marijuana and masturbation and motor bikes are as good as cricket and gardening and playing with children.

But tastes cannot be treated as an autonomous and independent entities. They develop and grow in a social context in which the state can, and usually does, have an important influence. The state has a purpose, in the last analysis, only in providing the conditions for its people to lead satisfying and meaningful lives. It has no choice but to affect 'taste'; its ultimate purpose requires it to play its part in the formation of desire.

My argument is deeply hostile to the premises of much liberal thought. Liberals ought to be shocked by it. For instance, cricket is a profound and absorbing activity, closely attuned to man's spiritual needs. Albert Camus said that most of what he had learnt that was of moral significance was learnt on the football field. But Camus had no knowledge of cricket, a game in which technique and teamwork and planning strategically to win, often by adapting more quickly to the land and the weather, are taken to their highest levels. Of course, cricket can be boring and silly, but it can also be profound and deeply satisfying and it has fewer disadvantages than war. Should cricket, then, be compulsory? In principle and up to a point, yes. Where it would work and not cause a reaction against the activity itself, children should be obliged to make some acquaintance with cricket, as with music. But this would not work where cricket is alien to a culture, nor with individuals who have begun to react against it. Thus it should only be compulsory in a very limited sense for some children in some cultures. In any case, there are other activities with spiritual qualities and it may be more efficient that individuals find their own. These are questions of judgement; there is no question of a philosophic ban on interference with matters of taste.

It is not, of course, a plausible objective of political philosophy to specify precisely how people should spend their leisure time, to prescribe (for instance) universal compulsory cricket. Societies can thrive without cricket; in the interests of cultural diversity it is desirable that they do. Within a cricket-playing society decent individuals can live rich lives while abhorring the game. But cricket is not entirely irrelevant to political philosophy. It is the *kind* of activity which gives people's lives meaning and makes them satisfying. Whether or not people's tastes are directed to such activities and whether or not suitable opportunities are available to them is in part, but necessarily, a consequence of the decisions of governments.

There is thus some necessary connection between policy and the meaning of life, but the connection is subtle and indirect. It is like steering a ship with a broken rudder and no engine; the state may fail to exercise any control over the meaning of its citizens' lives, but it ought not to refrain from trying. However, its control could only ever be a matter of detailed incremental policy in fields like education, environmental planning and industrial development. There is no question of the Life (meaning of) Act, 1999.

However, in some general respects my idea of the meaning of life has anti-humanist implications. A world without differences of race, class and nation, a world without ownership, competition, and dynasty, would be boring and meaningless. It would lack a sense of the particular and a sense of humour. It is not just that the great dreams of a world of peace and equality and the satisfaction of basic needs and abolition of sources of disharmony are unattainable, nor even that they are dangerous because they encourage fanaticism and destruction. Most conservatives accept these arguments, but do not go beyond them. Even if attained, such dreams offer a life which would be boring and meaningless, in which we could not be ourselves, but would be mere 'persons'. The more fanatical forms of humanism even threaten the sensual pleasures by giving them (for instance, sex and the enjoyment of landscape) an ideological status which makes the pleasure dangerous and trivial.

There is an important paradox, concerning the Fall and its secular implications. Conservatives are said to believe in the Fall, in that they believe that man is irredeemably corrupt and selfish. But some conservatives, at least, accept and love the world for what it is, not judging it as a whole and not expecting it to be better or worse than it is. Conversely, much humanist and critical thought is based on the premise that existing societies *are* wicked and corrupt by some standard which can be applied to the whole and which implies the inadequacy of our existing society. At their best, such traditions are a powerful and constructive force for social improvement. At their worst, they degenerate into a religion which is both millenarian and puritanical, which allows no pleasure in food while anyone is starving and sees all human action as trivial unless it contributes to the radical transformation of society. This kind of philosophy wishes life away; the career of 'humanity' will be over before it is begun. Conservatism, on the other hand, for all its scepticism and pessimism, must also be premised on some affection for life as it really is and a belief that it is, for the most part, worth living.

BIBLIOGRAPHY

Adams, Richard, *Watership Down*, Penguin, 1974

Allardt, Erik, *Implications of the Ethnic Revival in Modern, Industrial Society*, Commentationes Scientarum Socialum 12, Societas Scientarum Fennica, Helsinki, 1979

Ardrey, Robert, *African Genesis, A Personal Investigation into the Animal Origins and Nature of Man*, Collins, 1961

Arendt, Hannah, The Origins of Totalitarianism, revised ed., Allen and Unwin, 1967

Austin, J. L. *Philosophical Papers* (edited by J. O. Urmson and G. J. Warnock), Clarendon Press, 1961

Austin, J. L., *Sense and Sensibilia*, Clarendon Press, 1962

Ayer, A. J., *Language, Truth and Logic*, Gollancz, 1936

Ayer, A. J. (ed.), *Logical Positivism*, The Free Press, Glencoe, 1959

Bachrach, Peter, *The Theory of Democratic Elitism, a critique*, Little, Brown, 1967

Bachrach, Peter and Baratz, Morton, 'Two Faces of Power', *American Political Science Review*, vol. LVI, 1962

Bachrach, Peter and Baratz, Morton, *Power and Poverty, theory and practice*, OUP, 1970

Banfield, Edward, *The Unheavenly City, the nature and future of our urban crisis*, Little, Brown, 1968

Bantock, G. H., *Freedom and Authority in Education*, Faber and Faber, 1952

Beer, Samuel, *Modern British Politics*, Faber and Faber, 1965

Bentham, Jeremy, *Collected Works* (general editor J. H. Burns), University of London, Athlone Press, 1968–

Berlin, Isaiah, *Two Concepts of Liberty*, OUP, 1958

Brzezinski, Zbigniew and Friedrich, Carl, *Totalitarian Dictatorship and Autocracy*, Praeger, 1966

Burke, Edmund, *The Works* , OUP, 1907

Burnham, James, *The Managerial Revolution*, Indiana University Press, 1941

Camus, Albert, *The Rebel*, London, Penguin, 1962

Connolly, William, *The Terms of Political Discourse*, D. C. Heath, 1974

Dahl, Robert A., 'The Concept of Power', *Behavioural Science*, vol. 2, 1957

Dahl, Robert A., 'A Critique of the Ruling Elite Model', *American Political Science Review*, vol. 52, 1958

Dahl, Robert A., *Who Governs?*, Yale University Press, 1961

Dahl, Robert A., *Modern Political Analysis*, Prentice-Hall, 1963

Daniels, Norman (ed.), *Reading Rawls, critical studies on Rawls's* 'A Theory of Justice', Blackwell, 1975

Dawkins, Richard, *The Selfish Gene*, OUP, 1976

Dearden, R. F., Hirst, P. H. and Peters, R. S. (eds), *Education and the Development of Reason*, Routledge and Kegan Paul, 1972

Devlin, Patrick, *The Enforcement of Morals*, OUP, 1965

Dworkin, Ronald, *Taking Rights Seriously*, Duckworth, 1977

Eccleshall, Robert, 'English Conservatism as Ideology', *Political Studies*, vol. XXV, 1977

Filmer, Sir Robert, *Patriarcha and other political writings*, edited by Peter Laslett, Blackwell, 1949

Friedman, Milton, *Capitalism and Freedom*, University of Chicago Press, 1962

Friedman, Milton and Friedman, Rose, *Free to Choose, a personal statement*, Secker and Warburg, 1980

Gallie, W. B., 'Essentially Contested Concepts', *Proceedings of the Aristotelian Society*, vol. LVI, 1955–56

Gramsci, Antonio, *Prison Notebooks (Quaderni del Carcere)*, selections from the prison notebooks, selected and translated by Quentin Hoare and Geoffrey Nowell-Smith, Lawrence and Wishart, 1971

Gribble, James, *Introduction to the Philosophy of Education*, Allyn and Bacon, 1969

Harrington, James, *The Political Works of James Harrington*, edited with an introduction by J. G. A. Pocock, Cambridge University Press, 1977

Hayek, F. A. von, *The Road to Serfdom*, Routledge, 1944

Hayek, F. A. von, *Studies in Philosophy, Politics and Economics*, Chicago University Press, 1967

Hirst, P. H. and Peters, R. S., *The Logic of Education*, Routledge and Kegan Paul, 1970

Hobbes, Thomas, *Leviathan* edited with an introduction by Michael Oakshott, Blackwell, 1955

Honoré, A. M., 'Ownership', in A. G. Guest (ed.), *Oxford Essays in Jurisprudence*, Clarendon Press, 1961

Hume, David, *The Philosophical Works*, edited by T. H. Green and T. H. Grose, Aalen, Scientia Verlag, 1964

BIBLIOGRAPHY 175

Hunter, Floyd, *Community Power Structure*, North Carolina University Press, 1953

Illich, Ivan, *Deschooling Society*, Harper and Row, 1973

Kant, Immanuel, *Critique of Pure Reason*, translated by Norman Kemp-Smith, Macmillan, 1929

Kant, Immanuel, *Critique of Practical Reason and other writings in moral philosophy*, translated and edited with an introduction by Lewis White Beck, Garland Publishing, 1976

Kropotkin, Prince Peter Aleksievich, *Mutual Aid*, Penguin, 1939

Kropotkin, Prince Peter Aleksievich, *The Essential Kropotkin*, edited by Emile Capouya and Keitha Tompkins, Macmillan, 1976

Kuhn, Thomas, *The Structure of Scientific Revolutions*, University of Chicago Press, 1962

Lammenais, Félicité Robert de, *De l'absolutisme et de la liberté et autres essais*; présenté par Henri Guillemi, Editions Ramsay, 1978

Laslett, Peter (ed.), *Philosophy, Politics and Society*, Blackwell, 1956

Laslett, Peter and Runciman, W. G. (eds), *Philosophy, Politics and Society*, Second Series, Blackwell, 1962

Lenin, V. I., *The State and Revolution*, Lawrence and Wishart, 1918

Livingstone, E. A. (ed.), *The Concise Oxford Dictionary of the Christian Church*, OUP, 1972

Locke, John, *Two Treatises of Government*, edited by P. Laslett, Cambridge University Press, 1964

Lukes, Steven, *Power: a radical view*, Macmillan, 1975

MacCallum, Gerald C. Jr., 'Negative and Positive Freedom', in Anthony de Crespigny and Alan Wertheimer (eds), *Contemporary Political Theory*, Nelson's University Paperbacks, 1971

Mackenzie, W. J. M., *Politics and Social Science*, Penguin, 1967

Mackenzie, W. J. M., *Biological Ideas in Politics*, Penguin, 1978

Maistre, Joseph de, *Works*, selected, translated and with an introduction by J. Lively, Allen and Unwin, 1965

March, James, 'The Power of Power', in David Easton (ed.), *Varieties of Political Theory*, Prentice-Hall, 1966

Marx, Karl, *Collected Works of Karl Marx and Frederick Engels*, Lawrence and Wishart, 1975–

Michels, Robert, *Political Parties*, The Free Press, Glencoe, 1949

Mill, John Stuart, *Collected Works*, University of Toronto Press, 1963–

Miller, David, *Social Justice*, Clarendon Press, 1976

Mills, C. Wright, *The Power Elite*, OUP, 1956

Mills, C. Wright, *The Sociological Imagination*, OUP, 1959

Mills, C. Wright, *Power, Politics and People, the collected essays of C. Wright Mills*, edited and with an introduction by Irving Louis Horowitz, OUP, 1963

Montesquieu, Charles Louis de Secondat, Baron de, *The Spirit of the Laws*, translated by T. Nugent, Hafner, 1949

Morris, William, *News from Nowhere*, Routledge and Kegan Paul, 1970

Mosca, Gaetano, *The Ruling Class*, McGraw-Hill, 1939

Nozick, Robert, *Anarchy, State and Utopia*, Blackwell, 1974

Oppenheim, Felix, *Political Concepts, a reconstruction*, Blackwell, 1981

Orwell, George, *1984*, Secker and Warburg, 1949

Paine, Thomas, *The Rights of Man*, Dent, 1969

Pareto, Vilfredo, *The Mind and Society*, Jonathan Cape, 1935

Polsby, Nelson, *Community Power and Political Theory, a further look at problems of evidence and inference*, Yale University Press, 1980

Pope, Alexander, *Poetical Works*, edited by Herbert Davis, OUP, 1978

Proudhon, Pierre, *Selected Writings*, edited with an introduction by Stewart Edwards, translated by Elizabeth Fraser, Macmillan, 1969

Quinton, Anthony, *The Politics of Imperfection: the religious and secular traditions of conservative thought in England from Hooker to Oakshott*, Faber, 1978

Rawls, John, *A Theory of Justice*, OUP, 1972

Riker, William and Ordeshook, Peter, *An Introduction to Positive Political Theory*, Prentice-Hall, 1972

Rousseau, Jean-Jacques, *The Social Contract and discourses*, translated by G. D. H. Cole, Dent, 1963

Rousseau, Jean-Jaques, *Emile or Education*, translated by Bernard Foxley, Dent, 1965

Russell, Bertrand, *Power: a new social analysis*, Allen and Unwin, 1938

Ryan, Alan, 'The Opium of the Marxists', *New Society*, vol. 62, 1982

Scruton, Roger, *The Meaning of Conservatism*, Penguin, 1980

Scruton, Roger, *A Dictionary of Political Thought*, Macmillan, 1982

Steiner, Hillel, 'Individual Liberty', *Proceedings of the Aristotelian Society*, vol. LXXV, 1974–75

Stevenson, C. L., *Ethics and Language*, Yale University Press, 1944

Strawson, Peter, *Individuals*, Methuen, 1959

Strawson, Peter, *The Bounds of Sense*, Methuen, 1966

Strawson, Peter, *Freedom and Resentment and other essays*, Methuen, 1974

Suetonius Tranquillus, Gaius, *The Twelve Caesars*, translated by Robert Graves, Penguin, 1957

Thucydides, *History of the Peloponnesian War*, translated by Robert Crawley, Dent, 1910

Toulmin, Stephen, *The Philosophy of Science*, Hutchinson, 1953

Tuckman, Barbara, *A Distant Mirror, The Calamitous Fourteenth Century*, Ballantine Books, 1978

Weber, Max, *From Max Weber: essays in sociology*, translated, edited and with an introduction by H. H. Gerth and C. Wright Mills, Routledge and Kegan Paul, 1964

White, J. P., *Towards a Compulsory Curriculum*, Routledge and Kegan Paul, 1973
Woodcock, George, *Anarchism*, Penguin, 1963
Woodcock, George (ed.), *The Anarchist Reader*, Fontana, 1977

INDEX

Illich, Ivan, 133

Jesus Christ, 63–4
Johnson, Samuel, 169

Kant, Immanuel, 53, 68
Keynes, J. M., 8, 13, 17, 45
Kropotkin, P. A., Prince, 31, 33–4, 36,
    85
Kuhn, Thomas, 58

Lammenais, F. R. de, 15
Laslett, Peter, 50–1
Lee Kwan Yew, 9
Lenin, V. I., 153
Locke, John, 3, 10, 14, 100, 109, 125
Lukes, Steven, 40, 141, 145–6

MacCallum, Gerald, 116
Mackenzie, W. J. M., 31, 40
Maistre, Joseph de, 15–16, 21
March, James, 40
Marx, Karl, 6, 30, 36, 100
Merton, Robert K., 36, 45
Michels, Robert, 39
Mill, John Stuart, 13, 120, 121, 160
Miller, David, 84–5
Mills, C. Wright, 146
Montesquieu, C. de S. de, 85, 152
Moore, Barrington, 154
Morris, William, 34, 36, 169
Mosca, Gaetano, 38
Mussolini, Benito, 39, 156

National Council for Civil Liberties,
    125
National Trust, 99, 108
Neill, A. S., 133
Newton, Isaac, 56, 58
Nozick, Robert, 14, 51–2, 54, 109

Oppenheim, Felix, 48–9

Ordeshook, Peter, 48
Orwell, George, 39

Paine, Thomas, 93
Pareto, Vilfredo, 39
Pericles, 162
Peters, R. S., 133
Plamenatz, John, 109
Polsby, Nelson, 140, 145
Pope, Alexander, 10, 11, 29
Proudhon, Pierre, 102

Quinton, Anthony, 30

Rawls, John, 25–6, 51–2, 54, 83
Reagan, Ronald, 157
Riker, William, 48
Rousseau, Jean-Jacques, 114, 116, 133,
    134
Runyon, Damon, 148
Russell, Bertrand, 38, 39, 51, 138
Ryan, Alan, 61–2

Scruton, Roger, 18, 109
Smith, Sydney, 85
Speight, Johnny, 11
Spencer, Herbert, 85
Stalin, Joseph, 22, 39, 74
Steiner, Hillel, 147
Stevenson, C. L., 43–4, 158
Strawson, Peter, 53
Suetonius, 31

Thatcher, Margaret, 162
Thucydides, 31, 159
Toulmin, Stephen, 56
Tuckman, Barbara, 29–30

Weber, Max, 60, 149
White, J. P., 133
Wilson, Harold, 157